The Alternative
to Capitalism

The Alternative
to Capitalism

Adam Buick and John Crump

THEORY AND PRACTICE

2018, 2017, 2013 Theory and Practice

www.theoryandpractice.org.uk

ISBN: 978-0-9956609-6-0

This book contains material first published in the books:
State Capitalism: The Wages System Under New Management (1986)
and
Non-Market Socialism in the Nineteenth and Twentieth Centuries (1987)

Third edition. Contains material omitted from previous versions.

Contents

Preface

According to conventional wisdom, in the 70 or so years following the Russian Revolution of 1917 the globe was divided into two 'worlds' – the 'capitalist' or 'free' world and the 'socialist' or 'communist' world. The principal characteristic of the 'capitalist' or 'free' world is that free market forces are supposed to shape its economies, while in the 'socialist' or 'communist' world the economies of the various countries were said to be planned.

These articles challenge this conventional wisdom. They argue that, given the nature of both capitalism and socialism, their coexistence is an impossibility. In today's conditions, what both capitalism and socialism have in common is their all-or-nothing quality. In other words, modern capitalism is necessarily a worldwide system of commodity production based on wage labour, and the level of production in all parts of the world is ultimately determined by the need of productive enterprises (no matter whether they are owned by individual entrepreneurs, are joint-stock companies or are state-managed concerns) to compete with rivals on the world market. Conversely, socialism could only come into existence by replacing capitalism throughout the world, so as to abolish the world market and institute a global system of production for use and not for sale.

No matter how sweeping the political changes which

occur within national frontiers, as long as world capitalism and nation-states persist, those who make decisions about production are compelled to respond to the forces of competition which are integral to the world market. This applies even in a country where all individual entrepreneurs have been eliminated and where all the means of production have been taken over by the state. Whatever the political coloration of the leadership in such a country, the state still has to act as a capitalist, owing to the pressures exerted by the world market system on that country's productive forces. Indeed, even in countries such as Britain, where private enterprise still operates, those same pressures exerted by the world market system have forced the state to take an active role in decisions which affect production. Thus even in avowedly 'capitalist' countries, the state has increasingly come to the fore, while in the supposedly 'socialist' countries the state actually became the capitalist for which the most accurate description is 'state capitalism'.

What is Capitalism?

To say that state capitalism is a variety of capitalism may be a tautology, but it brings out the need to be clear about what capitalism is before embarking on any discussion of what state capitalism may be. In this chapter we shall identify the essential features of capitalism and then go on to discuss state capitalism and the nature of the capitalist class. We shall be describing in Marxian terms, concisely but thoroughly, the economic mechanism and set of social relationships that constitute capitalism. We believe Marx's analysis to be in general still valid even if, the institutional forms of capitalism have changed from those of Britain in the nineteenth century which Marx studied. We can assure readers who may initially find parts of this chapter difficult that if they persevere they will acquire a basic understanding of the key concepts in Marxian economics which will not only allow them to follow better the other, less theoretical chapters but will also equip them to tackle the many other books and articles written these days from a general Marxist theoretical standpoint.

We shall suggest that, apart from being a class society, capitalism has the following six essential characteristics:

1. Generalised commodity production, nearly all

wealth being produced for sale on a market.

2. The investment of capital in production with a view to obtaining a monetary profit.

3. The exploitation of wage labour, the source of profit being the unpaid labour of the producers.

4. The regulation of production by the market via a competitive struggle for profits.

5. The accumulation of capital out of profits, leading to the expansion and development of the forces of production.

6. A single world economy.

Generalised commodity production

Capitalism is an exchange economy in which most wealth, from ordinary consumer goods to vast industrial plants and other producer goods, takes the form of commodities, or items of wealth that have been produced with a view to sale on a market.

Commodity production existed before capitalism but in previous societies was marginal to the predominant form of wealth production. In previous societies, such as feudalism, wealth was principally produced for direct use and not for sale on a market. Wealth was used by those who produced that wealth, or else by the privileged classes who lived off the producers and acquired wealth from them by the actual or threatened use of force. In capitalism the roles of production for sale and production for use are reversed; it is now production for use that is marginal, while the great bulk of wealth is produced for sale. In particular, the elements needed for producing wealth (raw materials, machines and human mental and physical energy) become commodities.

In an exchange economy, wealth is not produced for its own sake. Wealth, or useful things fashioned or refashioned by human beings from materials found in nature, is not produced to be directly available for some individual or social use, but is produced to be exchanged. To be exchangeable an item of wealth has to be of some use, otherwise no one would want to buy it, but it is not for this use value that it is produced. It is produced to be exchanged for other items of wealth, for its exchange value.

This distinction between use value and exchange value, between *wealth* and *value*, is a key concept for understanding how capitalism works. Value is not something completely distinct from wealth since it is the same labour which fashions or refashions the material found in nature into an object of use to human beings which, in an exchange economy, gives that object its exchange value. Value is a characteristic of wealth in an exchange economy, the form assumed by wealth in such an economy.

To say that it is labour that gives wealth exchange value is merely to say that this is how the labour involved in producing useful things expresses itself in a society where wealth is produced for sale rather than for use. It produces exchange value as well as use value. The labour theory of value can be seen as a corollary to what might be called a labour theory of wealth. Most wealth, as something useful that satisfies a human want, is produced by human beings transforming nature by their labour. Certain things, it is true, are useful to human beings without being the product of their labour – the sunlight and the air we breathe, for instance – but these 'gifts of nature' are precisely the only items of wealth which have no exchange value, are 'free goods' in an exchange economy.

The labour theory of value is not so much a theory of price as a theory of the nature of wealth in an exchange economy. Even so, it is possible to construct a theoretical model of an exchange economy in which commodities would exchange in proportion to the amount of average social labour-time needed to produce them. In such a model, commodities would be produced by independent producers owning their own means and instruments of production and exchanging their products for those of other producers in order to acquire the things they needed to live. This model is not, of course, capitalism, but it bears a resemblance to the type of exchange which took place on the margin of pre-capitalist societies.

In capitalism, on the other hand, where most of those engaged in production do not own means and instruments of production and where exchange takes place not simply to acquire use values but with a view to profit, commodities do not in fact exchange at their labour-time values. Rather they tend to sell at a price calculated by adding to their average social cost of production a percentage mark-up representing the going rate of profit. However, the sum total of the prices of all the commodities is still equal to their total value, those selling above their value compensating, as it were, for those which sell below it. In other words, in capitalism, the value price equation posited by the labour theory of value has validity only at the level of the whole economy.

Value is not measured directly in units of labour-time but in units of money. This is because the exchange value of a commodity is not the actual amount of labour-time embodied in it, but only that which is on average necessary to produce it, an average which can only be established through exchange, on the market. Money originated from barter, the simplest form of exchange, as the one commodity in which the exchange value of all the other commodities could be expressed and measured. To perform this role money itself had to have exchange value derived from being a product of labour; which enabled the money-commodity to act also as a store of value. Money still performs both these roles today, although this is heavily obscured by the subsequent evolution of money away from its original terms (principally gold and silver) to symbolic coins and paper notes.

In capitalism money comes to be the universal unit of economic calculation. It is, in fact, the only possible such unit, since there is no other way of comparing the endless variety of different kinds of wealth. Use values cannot be compared as such; only exchange values can and it is these that in the end money is measuring.

Investment of capital in production with a view to profit

We are now in a position to attempt a preliminary definition of *capital*, clearly a key concept for understanding the system to which it has given its name.

Capital, as a feature of an exchange economy, is a sum of exchange values, a stock not of wealth as such but of commodities, of wealth that has been produced for sale. Historically, capital has been regarded as being a stock of the money-commodity and it is easy to see why: capital is a sum and a stock of value of which money is both the measure and a store. But capital can also be, and generally is under capitalism, a stock or collection of other commodities whose exchange value is merely measured in monetary units.

Capital is no more simply a collection of exchange values than it is simply a stock of wealth; it is a collection of exchange values that is used to yield a monetary income. Capital is money which generates more money, or rather value which generates more value.

Capital, as money invested for profit, existed before the development of capitalism. Money lent for interest (usurer's capital) yielded its owner an income. Similarly, money invested in the sort of trading which involved buying in cheap markets or simply plundering and then selling in dear markets (the early form of merchant's capital) also brought in an income. But neither this interest nor this profit came from the capital having been invested in production. Certainly, ultimately, their source could only have been the labour of some producers, but this was not their direct source.

These two forms of capital played an important role in creating one of the historical preconditions for the development of capitalism as a system wherein capital is invested in production: the concentration into the hands of a small minority of sums of money looking for a profitable investment outlet. When the other preconditions were met – the formation of an international market, a certain development of the techniques of production permitting production on a larger scale than previously, but above all the separation of the producers from the means of production and the creation of a landless proletariat – this money was able to find the profitable outlet it was seeking by being invested in the actual production of wealth.

Thus, once capitalism has developed, capital can be defined either as money invested in production for profit or as wealth used to produce other wealth with a view to profit, both of which express the same idea from a different angle. A more rigorous, if more difficult, definition, whose full significance we will see later, would be that capital is value invested in production with a view to increasing itself, or self-expanding value.

Exploitation of wage labour

What is the source of the profit which accrues to capital invested in the production of wealth? How does this increase in exchange value, this extra or surplus value, come about?

The usurer obtained his profit out of the revenue of the persons he had lent his money to, and the merchant adventurer acquired his profit by cheating or plundering direct producers or other traders, but profit arises in a completely different way when capital is invested in the production of wealth. It is created within the process of production itself.

Under capitalism, as we saw, the elements needed for producing wealth become commodities; not only the raw materials and the machines but also the labour power of the producers. Labour power, or the mental and physical energy of human beings, has the particular property of being able to produce wealth when applied to nature-given materials. This property of labour power expresses itself in an exchange economy in the capacity to create new exchange value.

Labour power is not to be confused with labour, as is frequently done in everyday parlance when we talk about the 'labour market' and 'selling our labour'. Actually, At is not labour which is bought and sold on the labour market but labour power, the capacity to work. In fact labour, or work, cannot be sold since it cannot exist separately from the product in which it is embodied. Labour power is not the same thing as the product of labour. Indeed, it is precisely the difference between the values of these two separate commodities that is the key to the origin of surplus value.

The exchange value of labour power is roughly the cost of training, maintaining and replacing the particular kind of labour power concerned (skilled or unskilled, bricklayer or engineer, clerk or schoolteacher). Wages (or salaries) are its price, the monetary expression of its value.

Investing capital in production involves, first of all, converting it from money into the physical elements for producing wealth: into raw materials, into machinery and buildings, and into labour power. The workers, using the machines, expend their labour power to work the raw materials up into finished products. At the same time this expenditure of labour power creates new exchange value so that the total exchange value of the finished products is greater than the sum of the exchange values of the raw materials and of the wear and tear of the machines and buildings. Finally, the finished products are sold. When all the accounts are done, the original capital (now partly in the form of money, partly in the form of the machines and factory, but still a sum of values) is found to have increased in value.

Not all the new exchange value added in the process of production is profit since some of it has to be used to replace that part of the original capital which was invested in the purchase of labour power. In effect, the wage workers have worked a part of their time to replace the exchange value of their own labour power (represented by their wages) while the rest of the time they have worked for their employer for nothing. It is such unpaid labour that is the source of the surplus accruing to capital invested in the production of wealth.

Marx called the part of capital invested in the purchase of labour power 'variable capital' because it was the part of the total capital that, through the expenditure of the labour power, increased in value in the process of production. The other part, that invested in raw materials and in machinery and buildings, was 'constant capital' as its value was merely transferred unchanged to the product. The ratio of constant to variable capital was the organic composition of capital, while the ratio of surplus value to variable capital was the rate of surplus value or the rate of exploitation.

This process we have described is the exploitation of wage labour. It is exploitation even though it takes place fully in accordance with the normal rules of exchange so that nobody is cheated in the sense of not being paid the full price of what they have to sell. The workers receive as wages more or less the full exchange value of their labour power but, as we have pointed out, one property or use value of labour power is its ability to create new exchange value. This use value belongs to whoever purchases labour power and is theirs to use for their own purpose and benefit. The product and value which labour power produces belong to the purchaser of the labour power in question.

The exploitation of wage labour by capital is a defining feature of capitalism, reflecting the fact that capitalism is a class-divided society in which one class monopolises the means of production while the other, the vast majority, is forced to sell its mental and physical energies for wages in order to live. Capitalism is an exchange economy involving the buying and selling of labour power, a social system in which productive activity takes the form of wage labour. Wage labour and capital are two sides of one and the same social relationship. Wage labour, under conditions of generalised commodity production, inevitably produces capital as a sum of values accumulated out of surplus value, while the means of production can only function as capital by exploiting wage labour.[1] In this sense, capitalism could just as easily have come to be called 'the wages system' as 'the capitalist system'.

Production regulated by the competitive struggle for profits

An exchange economy such as capitalism implies not only that the various different kinds of wealth are produced by different producers in different places of work (a technical division of labour) but also, more importantly, that decisions about production are made by a number of autonomous economic units acting without reference to each other. Before goods can be exchanged they have to be regarded as belonging to some person, group of persons, or other subdivision of society. Exchange therefore implies the non-existence of the common ownership of the means and instruments of production that is the only basis on which decisions about production could be made

1 '...the relation between wage labour and capital determines the entire character of the mode of production. The principle agents of this mode of production itself, the capitalist and the wage worker, are to that extent merely personifications of capital and wage labour' (Marx, 1919 (vol. III) p. 1025). 'Capital and wage-labour (it is thus we designate the labour of the worker who sells his own labour power) only represents aspects of the self-same relationship' (Marx, 1979, p. 1006).

in a conscious coordinated manner.

In capitalism the 'autonomous economic units' which make decisions about production are profit-seeking exchange institutions which we shall call *enterprises*. An enterprise is an institution owning and controlling a separate capital. An enterprise may be a single individual or it may be a joint-stock company, a nationalised industry or even a workers' cooperative. It is not its internal structure that is important for understanding the role of the enterprise in capitalism hut rather the fact that it represents – incarnates, if you like – a separate capital, a separate sum of values seeking to expand itself through being invested in production.

All enterprises, whatever their legal status or internal structure, aim to increase the value of the capital they incarnate. This search for profit brings them into conflict with other enterprises, not just those engaged in producing the same or similar products but with every other enterprise, or rather with every other capital seeking to increase its value.

The origin of profits is, as we have seen, the unpaid labour of wage workers but this is not how it appears to enterprises. To them, profits are the difference between their production costs and their sales receipts and so appear to be made not in production but on the market. There is a sense in which this is true. The equation surplus value = profit is only valid for the economy as a whole, and it is the operation of the market which determines the share of surplus value going to the various competing enterprises as profits. Surplus value, in other words, is created in production but is won on the market as profits.

The total amount of profits that can be made by all

enterprises is thus limited by the total amount of surplus value that has been produced, but it is not the case that each enterprise makes profits equal to the amount of surplus value created by the workers it employs. If this were so, then, since labour alone is the source of new exchange value, labour-intensive industries would make the most profits; capital would therefore tend towards such industries and there would be no incentive to introduce labour-saving machines; which is patently contrary to what is observable under capitalism.

What happens in fact is that the competition between capitals tends to lead to each capital making a profit in proportion to its size; there is a tendency for the rate of profit – the ratio of the increase in value to the value of the original capital – to be the same in whatever line of production it is invested. It is as if the total amount of surplus value produced in all enterprises were pooled before being distributed to the individual capitals and as if enterprises, as incarnations of these capitals, competed to draw from this pool as much profit as they could. It is in this sense that the struggle between enterprises to make profits is in the end a struggle against every other enterprise: the more profits one enterprise makes the less there is left for the others.

If this competition between enterprises were completely unrestricted – if capitals could move rapidly and freely from one line of business to another – then each enterprise would make the same rate of profit on its capital; the amount of its profits would be directly related to the size of its capital. Such completely free competition and movement of capital has, of course, never existed, for political reasons (intervention of states) as well as for technical (minimum size of certain industrial plants) and economic (price-fixing and other monopolistic practices) ones. But it is still a tendency under capitalism as a system of competing capitals producing for sale on a changing market too large for any of them to control. Capitals, therefore, only tend to make the same rate of profit.

This tendency towards the averaging of the rate of profit explains why under capitalism commodities do not sell at their labour-time values but rather at a price equal to their cost of production plus a margin sufficient to allow the average rate of profit to be made on the total capital invested in their production.

In capitalism, then, decisions about production are in the hands of separate, competing capitals, be they large or small, privately owned or state controlled. However, this does not mean that production is completely unregulated. In any society there has to be some mechanism which regulates and coordinates decisions about production, otherwise it could not survive. In capitalism this regulating and coordinating mechanism is the market through which all enterprises are linked in a network of buying and selling transactions. This is the case because all enterprises enter the market not only as sellers of what their workers have produced, but equally as buyers of the elements for producing wealth (raw materials, machines, labour power). It is through prices, and particularly through changes in prices, that the market influences the decisions of enterprises concerning production. The worldwide market under capitalism is not fixed and stable. Even if it tends to expand in the long run, its condition at any particular time is unpredictable and liable to fluctuate.

Each enterprise makes its decisions about what, how

much and where to produce, how many workers to employ, the stocks of raw materials and finished products it should hold, what kinds of energy to use, whether or not to expand productive activity and so on, in the Light of the market prices of the commodities it has to buy or sell and on the basis of uncertain predictions as to how these might change. If the selling price of a commodity increases, then the enterprises engaged in producing that commodity will initially make bigger profits and so will be induced to increase their output; new enterprises may even enter the industry. On the other hand, if prices – and hence profits – are falling, then output will be curtailed.

The equilibrium position which the operation of the market tends to bring about (but which, of course, is never reached since the market is always changing) would be one in which the productive resources of society would be distributed in such a way that the enterprises engaged in producing the multitude of different items of wealth each made the same rate of profit on their capital.

We are not saying that the market is entirely independent of the actions of men and women, even if it does confront them as an external force. The market itself is in the end only the sum of the decisions to buy and sell made by enterprises and other actors in the capitalist exchange economy (wage-earners, states). What we are saying, however, is that individual decisions of this sort bring about results which no one has consciously willed and which narrowly limit the freedom of choice of enterprises — and indeed states — when making subsequent decisions about production.

Adam Smith spoke of this unplanned regulating and coordinating mechanism as being the work of an 'invisible hand'; Karl Marx called it 'the law of value'; popular language simply speaks of 'market forces'. All three expressions bring out the same idea: that production under capitalism is not consciously coordinated, but is determined by forces operating independently of people's will. Even though market forces are ultimately the result of a multitude of individual human decisions, nevertheless they confront people as external and coercive economic laws.

The accumulation of capital out of profits

The battle of competition between enterprises is fought by cheapening commodities, by enterprises trying to increase their share of the market by underselling their competitors.

It is true that, if they get the chance, enterprises will increase their profits by raising their prices, but they are not normally in a position to do this and, even when they are, it is not a lasting situation (unless supported by a state). Nor can enterprises increase their profits by permanently depressing the prices of the elements of production they buy (raw materials, wages, etc.), though again they will do so if, and for as long as, they get the chance.

Given, then, that enterprises normally have to accept the prices established by the market, the only way that they can compete against their rivals is to reduce their costs of production through improving the productivity of their workforce. Productivity is a measure of the number of articles of wealth as use values that can be produced in a given period of time. An increase in productivity means that more can be produced in the same period so that the cost per individual article, or unit-cost, falls. In value terms, the price of the commodity falls because less average social labour-time is required to produce it.

Productivity can be improved in a number of ways:

by getting the workers to work more intensively, by a better organisation of the process of production, but above all by employing more and better machines and techniques of production.

So the battle of competition comes to be fought by enterprises increasing their productivity so as to be able to sell more cheaply than their rivals. Whether an enterprise adopts an aggressive or a defensive approach in this battle, the result is the same: all enterprises are forced to invest in new and better machines. Once one enterprise has put itself in a position to undersell its competitors through having adopted some new cost-reducing technique, then the other enterprises are obliged to defend themselves by adopting the same new technique. Competition obliges all enterprises to run fast just to stand still; to remain in the race for profits, enterprises must stay competitive and to stay competitive they must continually increase their productivity, continually invest in new equipment. The weaker enterprises are pushed out of the market and eliminated from the struggle for profits, their capital passing into the hands of other enterprises.

This battle is fought throughout the worldwide capitalist economy in all industries. Investment in more and better machines to improve productivity is imposed on all enterprises by their competitive struggle for profits and as a price of their survival as a separate capital. The end result is twofold: the concentration of capitals into larger and larger units and a build-up of the stock and productive power of the instruments of production.

In capitalism this growth of the stock of instruments for producing wealth is at the same time an increase in the sum of exchange values, an accumulation of capital. The competitive struggle between capitals leads not only to capitals increasing their value, through the enterprises in which they are incarnated making profits out of producing wealth, but also to the reinvestment of this surplus value in production. This dynamic of capitalism results not simply in the expansion of production but also provides the stimulus for technical development.

Once again, this is not a matter of choice, but is something which is imposed on economic decision-makers as an external and coercive law. Enterprises are forced to accumulate the bulk of their profits as new capital by the same mechanism which regulates production under capitalism. Indeed, the accumulation of capital is part of this mechanism, since to accumulate capital is to allocate a portion of society's productive resources to expanding the stock of the means of production. This imperative to accumulate is, in fact, the dynamic of capitalism.

In regulating and coordinating production under capitalism, the competitive struggle between capitals decrees that priority shall be given to the expansion of the means of production over the consumption not only of the producers but also of those who personify capital. Capitalism is not a system which gives priority to the production of profits for the personal consumption of those who monopolise the means of wealth production; it is a system where the bulk of the profits made from investing capital in production are reinvested in production. The aim of capitalist production is not so much profits as the accumulation of capital.

We can now see the logic of defining capital impersonally as self- expanding value. The expansion of value and its accumulation as new capital is something that is imposed on men and women irrespective of their will. Capital is a product of people's labour which has escaped from their control and has come to dominate them in the form of coercive economic laws which they have no alternative but to obey and apply.

The accumulation of capital does not proceed in a smooth and continuous way; the graph of growth under capitalism is not an unbroken upward line but a series of alternating peaks and troughs in which each successive peak is usually (but not necessarily) higher than the previous one, so that the overall trend is upward. The growth of production under capitalism is cyclical, an ever-repeating series of periods of boom, overproduction, slump and recovery. This too is an inevitable result of the competitive struggle for profits and could be included as a feature of capitalism.

A world economy

One of the preconditions for the development of capitalism as a mode of production was the coming into being of a world market, or more accurately of an international market, since there was no need for the market system to have embraced the whole world before capitalism could develop. It was only necessary that the market should have embraced a number of countries specialising in the production of different kinds of wealth.

Capitalism came into being in Europe in the sixteenth century and continued to spread geographically until by the end of the nineteenth century it had come to embrace the whole world. This meant that it had become a world system in the full sense of the term, not simply an international system embracing a part of the globe within a single division of labour and a single exchange economy, but a world system embracing virtually all areas and all states.

This reflected the fact that the division of labour had become worldwide and that from then on all parts of the world were linked together in a single economic system via world trade and the world market. Capitalism had become a worldwide economic system. Indeed, capitalism could even be defined today as the world market economy.

This means that the economic laws of capitalism outlined in the previous sections operate on the world scale. Capitalism does not exist within the political boundaries of single countries; world capitalism is not a collection of separately existing national capitalisms but a single economic unit. Capitalism only exists on the world level, as a world economic system. There is no such thing as a 'national capitalist economy' and there never was. What this term seeks to describe is in fact only a section of the world economy that is subject to the control of one particular political unit, or state. It is this political division of the world into states, each with the power to issue its own currency, impose tariffs, raise taxes, pay subsidies and so on, that has given rise to the illusion that, rather than there being one world economy, there are as many 'national economies' as there are states. But this is only an illusion. There is only one capitalist system and it is worldwide.

A state can be defined as a law-making and law-enforcing institution having a monopoly of the legal use of force within a given geographical area. It is thus an instrument of political control, but states use their powers to play an economic role within capitalism. Up till now we have only mentioned this role in passing even though in fact states are just as much actors in the capitalist exchange economy as enterprises. This was deliberate since it is not possible to understand the economic role of states, even within their own frontiers, without having first realised that capitalism is a single international – now world – economic system embracing a number of separate political units.

Ever since capitalism came into existence states have intervened in the world market, to try to distort it in favour of enterprises operating from within their borders. They have used their political power to help their 'home' enterprises acquire a bigger share of world profits at the expense of enterprises operating from other countries. They have, for instance, imposed taxes on goods entering from outside their frontiers, in order to protect home enterprises from 'foreign' competition. They have, by diplomatic and by military means, sought to acquire protected foreign markets for home enterprises and, on the cost side, they have bargained and used force to acquire cheap raw materials for home industry. These interventions by states have led to periodic wars which can thus be included as another inevitable feature of capitalism.

Even so, states can only distort the world market to a limited extent. In making decisions that affect production within their frontiers they have to accept, just like any private enterprise, the pressures of the world market as external, coercive forces to which they must submit, if the capitals operating from within their frontiers are to survive in the battle of competition. Basically, they too must give priority to keeping costs down, in particular through productivity being continuously improved; to do this they must encourage the reinvestment of the greater part of profits in new, more productive machinery and plant, and they must limit the consumption of the wage-working class to what is necessary to maintain an efficient workforce. The internal political structure of a country makes no difference in this respect. Whether a country has a government which is elected by a majority of voters drawn from the wage-working class or whether its government is a brutal dictatorship, its state still has in the end to pursue policies dictated by the economic laws of capitalism.

State capitalism

Although states have intervened in capitalism ever since it came into existence, in so far as the aim was merely to interfere with the operation of world market forces, their intervention was only at the level of the division, not the production, of surplus value. However, over the past 100 or so years, there has been a definite trend in capitalism for states to go beyond merely trying to distort the world market, and to involve themselves in the actual production of wealth by establishing and operating state enterprises. In some countries, indeed in a large number outside what can be called the core area of world capitalism represented by North America, Western Europe and Japan, state ownership and state enterprise have become the predominant form.

In defining capitalism as a form of social organisation, now worldwide, in which production is carried on by wage labour and orientated towards the accumulation of capital via profits realised on the market, we deliberately left open the question of the form of ownership of the means of production — by private individuals, by joint-stock companies, by the state or even by cooperatives — since this is not relevant to the operation of the economic mechanism of capitalism. The substitution of state for private (individual or corporate) ownership does not mean the abolition of capitalism, since it leaves unchanged commodity production and both wage labour and the accumulation of capital.[2] It merely means that capital, or a part of the capital, in the political area of the world concerned has come to be incarnated by the state, or rather, in practice, by a number of different state enterprises.

The most appropriate term for describing this situation is *state capitalism*. Those countries where the most important means of production are state owned can be described as 'state capitalist countries'. However, it must be clearly understood that state capitalism is merely an institutional arrangement within world capitalism and that it can no more exist as a separate economic and social system in single countries than can any form of capitalism. The state capitalist countries do not exist apart from the rest of world capitalism; they are an integral part of it, one where state ownership and state enterprise have become the predominant institutional form for the operation of the economic mechanism of capitalism. This point has been well brought out by Immanuel Wallerstein:

> The capitalist system is composed of owners who sell for profit. The fact that an owner is a group of individuals rather than a single person makes no essential difference. This has long been recognised for joint-stock companies. It must now also be recognised for sovereign

2   'Where the state is itself a capitalist producer, as in exploitation of mines, forests, etc., its product is a "commodity" and hence possesses the specific character of every other commodity' (Marx, 1972, p. 51). In volume II of *Capital* Marx also refers in passing to 'state capital, so far as governments employ productive wage-labour in mining, railroading, etc. and perform the function of capitalists' (Marx, 1919 (vol. II), p. 110).

states. A state which collectively owns all the means of production is merely a collective capitalist firm as long as it remains – as all such states are, in fact, presently compelled to remain – a participant in the market of the capitalist world-economy. No doubt such a 'firm' *may* have different modalities of internal division of profit, but this does not change its essential economic role *vis-à-vis* others operating in the world market. (Wallerstein, 1979, pp. 68—9 – emphasis in original)

Though it is possible to imagine a state capitalist country organising itself as a single 'collective capitalist firm' to compete on the world market, in practice the state capitalist countries which exist today, such as Russia and China, have chosen to set up, to manage the accumulation of capital in the political area they control, not one, but a considerable number of state enterprises, each enjoying a certain amount of autonomy.

Who are the capitalist class?

Previously we argued that production is not carried on under capitalism for the benefit of those people who monopolise the means of social wealth production. On the contrary, we argued that the economic laws of capitalism ensure that people in this position accumulate as new capital the greater part of their profits. Nevertheless, these people still enjoy a privileged position with regard to consumption. Economically, they personify capital and act as its agents in the economic process; socially, they constitute a privileged, exploiting class. While, at the level of theoretical models, it is possible to imagine a situation in which personifying capital and enjoying a privileged consumption would not be linked, history has not produced any lasting example of this. In practice, the two have always been associated.

In those countries where capitalism first developed, those who have generally personified capital have been individual owners, people with a legal property title to all or part of the capital of an enterprise. Such people receive a legal property income in the form of interest or dividends and are able to transmit their property rights to their heirs. Some of those who have discussed the nature of capitalism have wanted to make the existence of a class of such individually-owning legal property title holders a defining feature of capitalism.[3] But this would be to make a fetish of a mere legal form.

Capitalism is a form of social organisation and, in analysing social formations, what is important are the actual social relationships that exist between the members of society rather than the legal property forms. Certainly, property forms tell us something about the way a society is organised, but they are not the most important element. At best they only reflect the real social relationships; at worst they disguise or distort them.

The basic social relationship of capitalism is that between capital and wage labour, that is to say between

3   For instance, James Burnham: 'Capitalist economy is a system of *private* ownership, of ownership of a certain type vested in private individuals, of private enterprise' and 'A capitalist is one who, as an individual has ownership interest in the instruments of production; entitled to the products of their labour' (Burnham, 1945, pp. 92 and 103 – emphasis in original). Burnham inherited this position, which was also that of Trotsky, from the orthodox Trotskyist movement from which he came. It is still the position of orthodox Trotskyism as well as of the official ideology of the Russian state.

those who in social practice personify capital and those who produce wealth for wages. Those who personify capital are those who, for a separate capital, have the ultimate responsibility for taking decisions about production. To be in this position they must effectively have exclusive decision-making powers in respect of an enterprise and the capital it represents; they must have a *de facto* control over the use of the means of production concerned. In the end, this control, since it involves the exclusion both of the producers and of those who personify other capitals, can only rest on the sanction and backing of a state, i.e. on physical force.

Legal property rights involve such a backing, since such rights are enforceable by the courts, the police and ultimately by the armed forces of a state. But it is quite possible for *de facto* control over the use of means of production to assume other forms than legal property rights. Let us suppose that, as a result of some political upheaval, individual property rights in a country were to be suppressed and that formal ownership of all the means of production was vested in the state. Who, in these circumstances, would personify capital? The answer to this question would be, as before, those who had the ultimate responsibility for taking decisions about the use of the means of production. These people would personify capital even if they happened to be a group which exercised *de facto* control collectively, rather than individually as in the case of legal property title holders. It might be the case that the identity of these people could only be established by an empirical study of the precise structure of the state, the institution in which capital would be incarnated under the circumstances, but they would be whichever group was found to control effectively the state.

Naturally, in these circumstances, the privileged consumption associated with personifying capital would be distributed in a different way than in those countries where it is individual property owners who personify capital. Here again, discovering in what precise way this was done would depend on an empirical study of the social facts but it would no longer be in the form of a legal property income (rent, interest, profit, dividend).

In other words, capital does not necessarily have to be personified by individually-owning legal property title holders. In fact, even in countries where this is so, this personification is no longer strictly individual, as it originally was. In the early days of capitalism, capital was widely personified by an individual, the private entrepreneur, who was certainly a legal property owner but for whom there was no distinction between his personal wealth and that of his enterprise. His profits belonged to him personally, just as he stood to lose all his personal wealth if his enterprise lost out in the battle of competition.

However, in the middle of the nineteenth century, the legal concept of limited liability was introduced (or rather was extended from a few privileged corporations to all business enterprises which claimed it). By this means enterprises acquired their own legal identity separate from that of the individual property owners who supplied their capital. This allowed the shareholders to keep the rest of their personal wealth if the enterprise foundered, but it also meant that the enterprise had become a separate legal entity in its own right. Capital, in other words, had become personified in an institution rather than in an individual. Corporate capital had come into being alongside individual capital.

An institution is a group of individuals organised in a particular way, so it is possible to discover who, in any institution, has ultimate responsibility for taking decisions, but the important point is that the existence of enterprises as separate legal institutions shows that capital does not have to be personified by individuals as individuals. Once this is admitted, then there can be no difficulty in accepting that capital can be personified by a state, or, more accurately, by those who control it. State capital is just as possible as corporate capital.

The two most significant types of enterprise in the world today are the limited liability company and the nationalised or state industry. These are the two main institutional forms in which the major competing capitals are incarnated throughout the world. Although the internal structure of enterprises is irrelevant when it comes to understanding how capitalism works as an economic system, it is crucial for identifying those who personify capital, those who fulfil the role of capitalist class, in any particular situation.

A member of the capitalist class can be defined as someone who, either as an individual or as a member of some collectivity, has ultimate responsibility for taking decisions about the organisation of production by wage labour for sale with a view to profit and who, again either individually or as part of a collectivity, enjoys a privileged consumption derived from surplus value. In short, a member of the capitalist class is someone who has ultimate responsibility for organising the accumulation of capital out of surplus value and who profits from this process. This permits a wide range of institutional arrangements, of which the private capitalist enjoying individual property rights vested in him as an individual is but one historical example. Capital can be, and has in fact been, personified by a wide variety of individuals and groups.

The Alternative to Capitalism

If state capitalism is not socialism, what is? In other words, if state ownership and management of production does not amount to the abolition of capitalism but only to a change in the institutional framework within which it operates, what would be the essential features of a society in which capitalism had been abolished?

Although it is possible to imagine that capitalism could be replaced by some new form of class society in which some other method of exploitation would replace the wages system, we shall concern ourselves here only with the replacement of capitalism by a society from which, to remain deliberately vague for the moment, exploitation and privilege would be absent.

Since capitalism is a worldwide class society and exchange economy, it is clear that the exploitation-less alternative to capitalism would have to be a classless world society without exchange.

No classes, no state, no frontiers

The basis of any society is the way its members are organised for the production of wealth. Where a section of society controls the use of the means of production, we can speak of a class society. Control of the means of production by a class implies the exclusion of the rest of society from such control, an exclusion which ultimately depends on the threatened or actual use of physical force. An institutionalised organ of coercion, or state, is thus a feature of all class societies and historically first made its appearance with the division of society into classes.

In all class societies, one section of the population controls the use of the means of production. Another way of putting this is that the members of this section or class own the means of production, since to be in a position to control the use of something is to own it, whether or not this is accompanied by some legal title deed.

It follows that a classless society is one in which the use of the means of production is controlled by all members of society on an equal basis, and not just by a section of them to the exclusion of the rest. As James Burnham put it:

> For a society to be 'classless' would mean that within society there would be no group (with the exception, perhaps, of temporary delegate bodies, freely elected by the community and subject always to recall) which would exercise, as a group, any special control over access to the instruments of production; and no group receiving, as a group, preferential treatment in distribution. (Burnham, 1945, p. 55)

In a classless society every member is in a position to take part, on equal terms with every other member, in deciding how the means of production should be used. Every member of society is socially equal, standing in exactly the same relationship to the means of production as every other member. Similarly, every member of society has access to the fruits of production on an equal basis.

Once the use of the means of production is under the democratic control of all members of society, class ownership has been abolished. The means of production can still be said to belong to those who control and benefit from their use, in this case to the whole population organised on a democratic basis, and so to be commonly owned by them. Common ownership can be defined as:

> A state of affairs in which no person is excluded from the *possibility* of controlling, using and managing the means of production, distribution and consumption. Each member of society can acquire the *capacity*, that is to say, has the opportunity to realise a variety of goals, for example, to consume what they want, to use means of production for the purposes of socially necessary or unnecessary work, to administer production and distribution, to plan to allocate resources, and to make decisions about short term and long term collective goals. Common ownership, then, refers to every individuals potential ability to benefit from the wealth of society and to participate in its running. (Bragard, 1981, p. 255 emphasis in the original)

Even so, to use the word ownership can be misleading in that this does not fully bring out the fact that the transfer to all members of society of the power to control the production of wealth makes the very concept of property redundant. With common ownership no one is excluded from the possibility of controlling or benefiting from the use of the means of production, so that the concept of property in the sense of exclusive possession is meaningless: no one is excluded, there are no non-owners.

We could invent some new term such as no-owner-ship and talk about the classless alternative society to capitalism being a no-ownership society, but the same idea can be expressed without neologism if common ownership is understood as being a social relationship and not a form of property ownership. This social relationship equality between human beings with regard to the control of the use of the means of production can equally accurately be described by the terms classless society and democratic control as by common ownership since these three terms are only different ways of describing it from different angles. The use of the term common ownership to refer to the basic social relationship of the alternative society to capitalism is not to be taken to imply therefore that common ownership of the means of production could exist without democratic control. Common ownership *means* democratic control *means* a classless society.

When we refer to the society based on common ownership, generally we shall use the term socialism, though we have no objection to others using the term communism since for us these terms mean exactly the same and are interchangeable. If we have opted for the term socialism this is as a means of showing that we decisively reject the Leninist insertion of some sort of transitional society, wrongly called socialism, between capitalism and its classless alternative, generally called communism. For us socialism is communism, since both terms describe the society which immediately follows the abolition of capitalism.

Common ownership is not to be confused with state ownership, since an organ of coercion, or state, has no place in socialism. A class society is a society with a state because sectional control over the means of production and the exclusion of the rest of the population cannot be asserted without coercion, and hence without a special organ to exercise this coercion. On the other hand, a class-less society is a stateless society because such an organ of coercion becomes unnecessary as soon as all members of society stand in the same relationship with regard to the control of the use of the means of production. The exist-ence of a state as an instrument of class political control and coercion is quite incompatible with the existence of the social relationship of common ownership. State owner-ship is a form of exclusive property ownership which implies a social relationship which is totally different from socialism.

As we saw, common ownership is a social relation-ship of equality and democracy which makes the concept of property redundant because there are no longer any excluded non-owners. State ownership, on the other hand, presupposes the existence of a government machine, a legal system, armed forces and the other features of an institutionalised organ of coercion. State-owned means of production belong to an institution which confronts the members of society, coerces them and dominates them, both as individuals and as a collectivity. Under state own-ership the answer to the question who owns the means of production? Is not everybody or nobody as with common ownership; it is the state. In other words, when a state owns the means of production, the members of society remain non-owners, excluded from control. Both legally and socially, the means of production belong not to them, but to the state, which stands as an independent power between them and the means of production.

The state, however, is not an abstraction floating above society and its members; it is a social institution, and, as such, a group of human beings, a section of society, organised in a particular way. This is why, strictly speaking, we should have written above that the state confronts most members of society and excludes most of them from control of the means of production. For wherever there is a state, there is always a group of human beings who stand in a different relationship to it from most members of society: not as the dominated, nor as the excluded, but as the dominators and the excluders. Under state ownership, this group controls the use of the means of production to the exclusion of the other members of society. In this sense, it owns the means of production, whether or not this is formally and legally recognised.

Another reason why state ownership and socialism are incompatible is that the state is a national institution which exercises political control over a limited geographical area. Since capitalism is a world system, the complete state ownership of the means of production within a given political area cannot represent the abolition of capitalism, even within that area. What it does mean, and this has been one of the major themes of this book, is the establishment of some form of state capitalism whose internal mode of operation is conditioned by the fact that it has to compete in a world market context against other capitals.

Since today capitalism is worldwide, the society which replaces capitalism can only be worldwide. The only socialism possible today is world socialism. No more than capitalism can socialism exist in one country. So the common ownership of socialism is the common ownership of the world, of its natural and industrial resources, by the whole of humanity. Socialism can only be a universal society in which all that is in and on the earth has become the common heritage of all humankind, and in which the division of the world into states has given way to a world without frontiers but with a democratic world administration.

No exchange, no economy

Socialism, being based on the common ownership of the means of production by all members of society, is not an exchange economy. Production would no longer be carried on for sale with a view to profit as under capitalism. In fact, production would not be carried on for sale at all. Production for sale would be a nonsense since common ownership of the means of production means that what is produced is commonly owned by society as soon as it is produced. The question of selling just cannot arise because, as an act of exchange, this could only take place between separate owners. Yet separate owners of parts of the social product are precisely what would not, and could not exist in a society where the means of production were owned in common.

However, socialism is more than just not an exchange economy; it is not an economy at all, not even a planned economy. Economics, or political economy as it was originally called, grew up as the study of the forces which came into operation when capitalism, as a system of generalised commodity production, began to become the predominant mode of producing and distributing wealth. The production of wealth under capitalism, instead of being a direct interaction between human beings and nature, in which humans change nature to provide themselves with the useful things they need to live, becomes a process of production of wealth in the form of exchange value. Under this system, production is governed by forces which operate independently of human will and which impose themselves as external, coercive laws when men and women make decisions about the production and distribution of wealth. In other words, the social process of the production and the distribution of wealth becomes under capitalism an *economy* governed by *economic* laws and studied by a special discipline, *economics*.

Socialism is not an economy, because, in re-establishing conscious human control over production, it would restore to the social process of wealth production its original character of simply being a direct interaction between human beings and nature. Wealth in socialism would be produced directly as such, i.e. as useful articles needed for human survival and enjoyment; resources and labour would be allocated for this purpose by conscious decisions, not through the operation of economic laws acting with the same coercive force as laws of nature. Although their effect is similar, the economic laws which come into operation in an exchange economy such as capitalism are not natural laws, since they arise out of a specific set of social relationships existing between human beings. By changing these social relationships through bringing production under conscious human control, socialism would abolish these laws and so also the economy as the field of human activity governed by their operation. Hence socialism would make economics redundant.

What we are saying, in effect, is that the term exchange economy is a tautology in that an economy only comes into existence when wealth is produced for exchange. It is now clear why the term planned economy is unacceptable as a definition of socialism. Socialism is not the planned production of wealth as exchange value, nor the planned production of commodities, nor the planned accumulation of capital. That is what state capitalism aims to be. Planning is indeed central to the idea of socialism, but socialism is the planned (consciously coordinated) production of useful things to satisfy human needs precisely instead of the production, planned or otherwise, of wealth as exchange value, commodities and capital. In socialism wealth would have simply a specific use value (which would be different under different conditions and for different individuals and groups of individuals) but it would not have any exchange, or economic, value.

Conventional academic economics in the West rejects the definition of economics as the study of the forces which comes into operation when wealth is produced to be exchanged. But even on the alternative definition it offers that economics is the study of the allocation of scarce resources to meet some human needs[1] – socialism would not be an economy. For socialism presupposes that productive resources (materials, instruments of production, sources of energy) and technological knowledge are sufficient to allow the population of the world to produce enough food, clothing, shelter and other useful things, to

1   This leads to the basic assumption which economic analysis makes about the physical world. It is assumed that the fundamental feature of the economic world, the feature which gives rise to economic problems at all, is that goods are *scarce*. Very few things in the world, with the exception of air, water and (in some countries) sunshine, are available in unlimited amounts. It is because of scarcity that goods have to be shared out among individuals. If scarcity did not exist, then there would be no economic system and no economics (Stonier and Hague, 1980, p. 3 emphasis in original).

satisfy all their material needs.

Conventional economics, while denying that the potential for such a state of abundance exists, nevertheless admits that if it did this would mean the end, not only of 'the economy' as a system of allocating scarce resources but also of goods having an economic value and price; goods would simply become useful things produced for human beings to take and use, while economics as the study of the most rational way to employ scarce resources would give way to the study of how best to use abundant resources to produce free goods in the amounts required to satisfy human needs.[2] Significantly, the ideologists of state capitalism take up a basically similar position: if abundance existed, value, prices, money, markets and wages could be abolished but, since abundance does not yet exist and could not be brought into existence for some considerable time, all these categories of capitalism must continue.[3]

2   Abundance removes conflict over resource allocation since by definition there is enough for everyone, and so there are no mutually exclusive choices, no opportunity is forgone and there is no opportunity-cost. The golden age, a communist steady-state equilibrium, will have been reached. Gradual change, growth, will be simple and painless. The task of planning becomes one of simple routine; the role of economics is virtually eliminated. There is then no reason for various individuals and groups to compete, to take possession for their own use of what is freely available to all (Nove, 1983, p. 15). There would then be no *economic goods*, i.e., no goods that are relatively scarce; and there would hardly be any need for a study of economics or economizing. All goods would be *free goods*, like pure air used to be (Samuelson, 1980, p. 17 emphases in original).

3   Present productive forces are quite inadequate to provide the whole of mankind with up-to-date comfort (Mandel, 1968, p. 610). The necessity of a transition period follows precisely from the fact

As far as academic economics in the West is concerned, this question is not really one of fact but of definition. Scarcity is built into to its theoretical system in that it
regards a factor of production as being scarce so long as it
is not available in unlimited supply. Thus for it abundance
can only be a theoretical limiting case a situation where
land, capital and labour were all available, quite literally, for
the taking which could never exist in practice, so that by
definition scarcity would always exist. But this is a quite
unreasonable definition both of scarcity and of abundance.
Abundance is not a situation where an infinite amount of
every good could be produced (Samuelson, 1980, p. 17).
Similarly, scarcity is not the situation which exists in the
absence of this impossible total or sheer abundance.
Abundance is a situation where productive resources are
sufficient to produce enough wealth to satisfy human
needs, while scarcity is a situation where productive
resources are insufficient for this purpose.

In any event, value and its categories do not arise
from scarcity as a supposed natural condition; they arise, as
we saw, from the social fact that goods are produced as
commodities. Similarly, socialism is not a mere state of
abundance; it is a social rather than a physical or technical
condition. It is the set of social relationships correspond-
ing to a classless society, i.e. to a society in which every

that on the morrow of the abolition of capitalism, *society is still living
in a situation of relative shortage of consumer goods*. The allocation of
consumer goods during the epoch of transition from capitalism to
socialism must therefore be effected essentially through exchange,
that is, through buying and selling. Consumer goods continue to be
commodities. Leaving aside the social wage, the labour force is
essentially paid in money. A huge monetary sector therefore
continues to exist in the economy (ibid., p. 632 emphasis in
original).

member stands in the same position with regard to controlling and benefiting from the use of the means of wealth production. The establishment of a classless society means an end to the wage labour/capital relationship which is the basic social relationship of capitalist society. The wage (or employment) relationship expresses the fact that control over the use of the means of production is exercised by a section only of society. It is a relationship between two social classes, presupposing a division of society into those who control access to the means of production and those who are excluded from such control and are obliged to live by selling their ability to work. Since the very existence of wage labour (employment) implies a class of owners and a class of non-owners of the means of production, no society in which the predominant form of productive activity continues to be wage labour can be regarded as being socialist.

In socialist society productive activity would take the form of freely chosen activity undertaken by human beings with a view to producing the things they needed to live and enjoy life. The necessary productive work of society would not be done by a class of hired wage workers but by all members of society, each according to their particular skills and abilities, cooperating to produce the things required to satisfy their needs both as individuals and as communities. Work in socialist society could only be voluntary since there would be no group or organ in a position to force people to work against their will.

Socialist production would be production solely for use. The products would be freely available to people, who would take them and use them to satisfy their needs. In socialism people would obtain the food, clothes and other articles they needed for their personal consumption by going into a distribution centre and taking what they needed without having to hand over either money or consumption vouchers. Houses and flats would be rent-free, with heating, lighting and water supplied free of charge. Transport, communications, health care, education, restaurants and laundries would be organised as free public services. There would be no admission charge to theatres, cinemas, museums, parks, libraries and other places of entertainment and recreation. The best term to describe this key social relationship of socialist society is *free access*, as it emphasises the fact that in socialism it would be the individual who would decide what his or her individual needs were. As to collective needs (schools, hospitals, theatres, libraries and the like), these could be decided by the groups of individuals concerned, using the various democratic representative bodies which they would create at different levels in socialist society. Thus production in socialism would be the production of free goods to meet self-defined needs, both individual and collective.

Calculation in kind

Under capitalism wealth is produced for sale, so that particular items of wealth (goods produced by human labour, useful things) become commodities which have an exchange value. Indeed, it is only as exchange value that wealth has significance for the operation of capitalism; all the millions of different kinds of useful things produced by human labour are reduced to a common denominator their economic value based ultimately on the average working time needed to produce them from start to finish, of which money is the measure. This enables them to be compared and exchanged with reference to a common

objective standard and also allows the calculations necessary to an exchange economy to be made in a common
unit.

With the replacement of exchange by common ownership what basically would happen is that wealth would
cease to take the form of exchange value, so that all the
expressions of this social relationship peculiar to an
exchange economy, such as money and prices, would auto-
matically disappear. In other words, goods would cease to
have an economic value and would become simply physical objects which human beings could use to satisfy some
want or other. This does not mean that goods would come
to have no value in any sense; on the contrary, they would
continue to have the physical capacity to satisfy human
wants. The so-called economic value which goods acquire
in an exchange economy has nothing to do with their real
use value as a means of satisfying wants, since the value of
a good to human beings, i.e. its capacity to satisfy some
want, has never borne any relation to the time taken to
produce it. In socialism goods would cease to be commodities but they would remain use values; indeed, with the
shedding of their useless economic value their importance
as use values would be enhanced, as this would be the sole
reason why they were produced.

The disappearance of economic value would mean
the end of economic calculation in the sense of calculation
in units of value whether measured by money or directly in
some unit of labour-time. It would mean that there was no
longer any common unit of calculation for making
decisions regarding the production of goods. This has
often been regarded as a powerful argument against socialism as a moneyless society, so powerful in fact that when it

was first expressed in a systematic way by Ludwig von Mises in 1920 (Hayek et al., 1935, pp. 87-130) it led many self-proclaimed Marxists, including Karl Kautsky, to abandon finally the definition of socialism as a value-less society (and thus, in effect, to recognise that they had always stood for state capitalism rather than socialism)[4] and others to elaborate complicated schemes for using labour-time as a common unit of account in socialism (GIC, 1930; Pannekoek, 1970, pp.23-9). Only one participant in the discussion, Otto Neurath, an academic on the margin of the German Social Democratic movement, pointed out that socialism, as a moneyless society in which use values would be produced from other use values, would need no universal unit of account but could calculate exclusively in kind.[5]

Calculation in kind is an essential aspect of the production of goods in any society, including capitalism. A commodity is, as we saw, a good which by virtue of being produced for sale has acquired in addition to its physical use value a socially-determined exchange value. Correspondingly, the process of production under capitalism is both a process of production of exchange values and a process of production of use values, involving two differ-

---

4   In the same way, even if people were to limit themselves strictly to the exchange of natural produce, the existence of money would continue to be indispensable in a socialist society as a measure of value for accounting purposes and for calculating exchange ratios (Kautsky, 1922, p. 318).

5   . . . the economic analysis, which starts off with quantities, which are measured differently, and which ends up with quantities, which are measured differently, can never be reduced to a single common denominator, especially not to the common denominator labour (Neurath, 1925, p. 74).

ent kinds of calculation. For the former, the unit of calculation is money, but for the latter there is no single unit but a whole series of different units for measuring the quantity and quality of specific goods used in the process of producing other specific goods (tonnes of steel, kilowatt-hours of electricity, person-hours of work and so on). The disappearance of economic or value calculation in socialism would by no means involve the disappearance of all rational calculation, since the calculations in kind connected with producing specific quantities of goods as physical use values would continue.

What it would involve would be the end of the subordination of the choice of which use values to produce and which technical methods to employ to exchange value considerations. In particular, the aim of production would cease to be to maximise the difference between the exchange value of the goods used up in the process of production and the exchange value of the final product.

One critic of socialism as a moneyless society, the Dutch academic and former minister, N. G. Pierson, writing in 1902 in reply to Kautskys talk On the Day After the Social Revolution (Kautsky, 1902), argued that, without the common unit of account represented by value as measured by money, socialist society would be unable to calculate its net income:

> We will now discuss the division of income and
> we will assume that this is effected according to
> the most advanced method, that of communism. We at once discover a value problem in the
> strict sense of the word. What is to be regarded
> as income, and what therefore comes into the
> question when considering the division? Natur-

ally only net income; but the income of the socialist State will also be gross income. Raw materials will be required for the goods which it manufacturers, and in the course of manufacture fuel and other things will be consumed and machines and tools will be wholly or partly worn out. The live stock which has been reared will have consumed fodder. In order to calculate its net income the communist society would therefore have to subtract all this from the gross product. But we cannot subtract cotton, coal and the depreciation of machines from yarns and textiles, we cannot subtract fodder from beasts. We can only subtract the value of one from the value of the other. Thus without evaluation or estimation the communist State is unable to decide what net income is available for division. (Hayek *et al*, 1935, p. 70)

Pierson was right: without economic value and money it would be impossible to calculate net income but this as the difference between the amount of exchange value in existence at the end as compared with at the beginning of a year is a calculation that would be quite unnecessary, indeed perfectly meaningless, in socialism. The aim of production in socialism being to produce concrete use values to satisfy human needs, all that could interest socialist society at the end of a year would be whether specific quantities of specific goods had been produced over that period. To check this there would be no need to reduce (to continue with Piersons examples) cotton, coal, machines, yarns, textiles, fodder and beasts, to some common unit; on the contrary, it is precisely in their concrete physical forms of cotton, coal and so on that socialist society would be interested in these goods and would want to count them.

Socialist society has no need for value computations such as net income, national income, gross national product and other such abstractions obtained by ignoring the concrete use values of the specific goods produced during a given period. Indeed, socialism involves precisely the freeing of production from its subordination to these exchange value considerations. The aim of production in socialism is not to maximise national income or GNP or growth (of exchange values), which are meaningless concepts for it, but to produce the specific amounts and kinds of use values which people had indicated they wanted to satisfy their needs. The calculations involved in organising and checking this would be calculations in kind and would not require any universal unit of measurement.

Similarly, at the level of the individual productive unit or industry, the only calculations that would be necessary in socialism would be calculations in kind. On the one side would be recorded the resources (materials, energy, equipment, labour) used up in production and on the other side the amount of the good produced, together with any by-products. This, of course, is done under capitalism but it is doubled by an exchange value calculation: the exchange value of the resources used up is recorded as the cost of production while the exchange value of the output (after it has been realised on the market) is recorded as sales receipts. If the latter is greater than the former, then a profit has been made; if it is less, then a loss is recorded. Such profit-and-loss accounting has no place in socialism and would, once again, be quite meaningless. Socialist production is simply the production of use values from use values, and nothing more.

Even though the existence of socialism presupposes conditions of abundance (i.e. where resources exceed needs) socialist society still has to be concerned with using resources efficiently and rationally, but the criteria of efficiency and rationality are not the same as they are under capitalism.

Under capitalism there is, in the end, only one criterion: monetary cost, which, as a measure of economic value, is ultimately a reflection of the average time taken to produce a good from start to finish. The managers of capitalist enterprises are obliged by the working of the market to choose the technical methods of production which are the cheapest, i. e. which minimise production time and therefore monetary cost. All other considerations are subordinate, in particular the health and welfare of the producers and the effects on the natural environment. Many commentators have long pointed out the harmful effects which production methods geared to minimising production time have on the producers (speed-up, pain, stress, accidents, boredom, overwork, long hours, shiftwork, nightwork, etc., all of which harm their health and reduce their welfare), while more recently scientists have documented the damage such production methods cause to nature (pollution, destruction of the environment and wildlife, exhaustion of non-renewable resources).

Socialism, as a society geared to producing only uses values and not exchange value, would take these other considerations into account and subordinate the choice of production methods to the welfare of human beings and the protection of their natural environment. No doubt this would lead in many cases to the adoption of production methods which, by capitalist standards, would be inefficient and irrational in the sense that were they to be adopted under capitalism they would cost more and so be unprofitable. This is why such methods are not adopted under capitalism, where it is exchange value and not use value that counts, and why capitalism would have to be replaced by socialism if the original aim of production as a means to serve and enhance human welfare were to be restored.

In socialism, men and women in the various industries and individual productive units would have the responsibility for producing given amounts of a particular good to a particular standard, would seek to minimise (ideally eliminate) the harm done to the health and welfare of human beings and to the environment. As there would thus be a clear object and clearly defined constraints, industries and productive units could use mathematical aids to decision-making such as operational research and linear programming to find the most appropriate technical method of production to employ. As neutral techniques these can still be used where the object is something other than profit maximisation or the minimisation of monetary costs.

As to decisions involving choices of a general nature, such as what forms of energy to use, which of two or more materials to employ to produce a particular good, whether and where to build a new factory, there is another technique already in use under capitalism that could be adapted for use in socialism: so-called cost-benefit analysis and its variants. Naturally, under capitalism the balance sheet of the relevant benefits and costs advantages and disadvantages of a particular scheme or rival schemes is drawn up in money terms, but in socialism a points system for attributing relative importance to the various relevant considerations could be used instead. The points attributed to these considerations would be subjective, in the sense that this would depend on a deliberate social decision rather than on some objective standard, but this is the case even under capitalism when a monetary value has to be attributed to some such cost or benefit as noise or accidents. Furthermore, in so far as money is an objective measure, what it measures is production time to the exclusion of all other factors. In the sense that one of the aims of socialism is precisely to rescue humankind from the capitalist fixation with production time/money, cost-benefit type analyses, as a means of taking into account other factors, could therefore be said to be more appropriate for use in socialism than under capitalism. Using points systems to attribute relative importance in this way would not be to recreate some universal unit of evaluation and calculation, but simply to employ a technique to facilitate decision-making in particular concrete cases. The advantages /disadvantages and even the points attributed to them can, and normally would, differ from case to case. So what we are talking about is not a new abstract universal unit of measurement to replace money and economic value but one technique among others for reaching rational decisions in a society where the criterion of rationality is human welfare.

Planning and industrial organisation
Socialism would inherit from capitalism the existing material basis: a complex worldwide productive network linking all the millions of individual productive units in the world (farms, mines, factories, railways, ships, etc) into a single

system. The links we are talking about are physical in the sense that one unit is linked to another either as the physical user of the others product or as the physical supplier of its materials, energy or equipment. Under capitalism such links are established in two ways: organisationally (as between different productive units forming part of the same private or state enterprise) and, above all, commercially (as when one enterprise contracts to buy something from, or to sell something to, another enterprise). In socialism the links would be exclusively organisational.

Planning in socialism is essentially a question of industrial organisation, of organising productive units into a productive system functioning smoothly to supply the useful things which people had indicated they needed, both for their individual and for their collective consumption. What socialism would establish would be a rationalised network of planned links between users and suppliers; between final users and their immediate suppliers, between these latter and their suppliers, and so on down the line to those who extract the raw materials from nature.

By industrial organisation we mean the structure for organising the actual production and distribution of wealth. Some activities, such as intercontinental transport and communications, the extraction of oil and of certain other key raw materials, developing the resources of the oceans, and space research, are clearly best treated at world level, and we can imagine them being organised by a World Transport Organisation, a World Raw Materials Board, a World Oceanic Regime and so on. To begin with, and assuming (as seems likely) that socialism would inherit a problem of world hunger from capitalism, the production of certain key foodstuffs and animal feedstuffs might also need to be organised on a world level; there already exists in the Food and Agriculture Organisation (FAO) a world body that could easily be adapted for this purpose.

There would be a need for an administrative and decision-making centre at world level, democratically controlled by delegates from the various regions of the socialist world (we say nothing of the size and limits of these regions since such details must be left to the members of socialist society to settle), whose basic task would be to coordinate relations between the world industrial organisations, between these and the world-regions, and between the various world-regions. This centre would not be a world government since, as we have already explained, there would be no state and no government, not even at world level, in socialism. It would be an administrative and coordinating body and would not be equipped with means of coercion.

Other industries, and in particular manufacturing and processing, could be organised at world-regional level. There is no point in drawing up in advance the sort of detailed blueprint of industrial organisation that the old IWW and the Syndicalists used to (despite the promising name of Industrial Workers of the World, these were in fact blueprints for industrial organisations within a national framework), but it is still reasonable to assume that productive activity would be divided into branches and that production in these branches would be organised by a delegate body. The responsibility of these industries would be to ensure the supply of a particular kind of product either, in the case of consumer goods, to distribution centres or, in the case of goods used to produce other goods, to productive units or other industries.

Since the needs of consumers are always needs for a specific product at a specific time in a specific locality, we will assume that socialist society would leave the initial assessment of likely needs to a delegate body under the control of the local community (although, once again, other arrangements are possible if that were what the members of socialist society wanted). In a stable society such as socialism, needs would change relatively slowly. Hence it is reasonable to surmise that an efficient system of stock control, recording what individuals actually chose to take under conditions of free access from local distribution centres over a given period, would enable the local distribution committee (for want of a name) to estimate what the need for food, drink, clothes and household goods would be over a similar future period. Some needs would be able to be met locally: local transport, restaurants, builders, repairs and some food are examples as well as services such as street-lighting, libraries and refuse collection. The local distribution committee would then communicate needs that could not be met locally to the body (or bodies) charged with coordinating supplies to local communities.

Once such an integrated structure of circuits of production and distribution had been established at local, regional and world levels, the flow of wealth to the final consumer could take place on the basis of each unit in the structure having free access to what is needed to fulfil its role. The individual would have free access to the goods on the shelves of the local distribution centres; the local distribution centres free access to the goods they required to be always adequately stocked with what people needed; their suppliers free access to the goods they required from the factories which supplied them; industries and factories free access to the materials, equipment and energy they needed to produce their products; and so on.

Production and distribution in socialism would thus be a question of organising a coordinated and more or less self-regulating system of linkages between users and suppliers, enabling resources and materials to flow smoothly from one productive unit to another, and ultimately to the final user, in response to information flowing in the opposite direction originating from final users. The productive system would thus be set in motion from the consumer end, as individuals and communities took steps to satisfy their self-defined needs. Socialist production is self-regulating production for use.

To ensure the smooth functioning of the system, a central statistical office would be needed to provide estimates of what would have to be produced to meet peoples likely individual and collective needs. These could be calculated in the light of consumer wants as indicated by returns from local distribution committees and of technical data (productive capacity, production methods, productivity, etc) incorporated in input-output tables. For, at any given level of technology (reflected in the input-output tables), a given mix of final goods (consumer wants) requires for its production a given mix of intermediate goods and raw materials; it is this latter mix that the central statistical office would be calculating in broad terms. Such calculations would also indicate whether or not productive capacity would need to be expanded and in what branches. The centre (or rather centres for each world-region) would thus be essentially an information clearing house, processing information communicated to it about production and distribution and passing on the results to industries for them to draw up their production plans so as to be in a position to meet the requests for their products coming from other industries and from local communities.

Impossibility of gradualism

The governments of some of the state capitalist countries, in particular those which had Leninism as their official ideology, used to proclaim as their long-term goal the establishment of a society which they call communism and which at first sight bears a resemblance to the society we have outlined as the alternative to capitalism. For instance, at its 22nd Congress in 1961, the Communist Party of the Soviet Union (CPSU) adopted a programme for the construction of communism. One of the many books and pamphlets produced to popularise this programme tells us:

> Communist distribution is a system of supplying members of society with all they need free of charge. In this society money will be superfluous. Under communism, consumer goods to say nothing of capital goods cease to be commodities. Trade and money will outlive themselves. Flats, cultural, communication and transport facilities, meals, laundries, clothes, etc., will all be free. Stores and shops will be turned into public warehouses where members of communist society will be supplied with commodities for personal use. The need for wages and other forms of remuneration will disappear. (Mans Dreams, 1966, pp. 172 and 224)

The society here described as communism is thus to be a

moneyless society, but there is an implication that there might still be a body separate from the members of society which would be handing out goods to them at its initiative. In other words, it is implied that the means of production might still be controlled by a minority group which would distribute products free to the excluded, non-controlling majority. That this is to be the case is confirmed by other passages in which we are told that communism can be established in one country or group of countries and that the party will continue to exist for a long time even after the establishment of communism on a world scale.[6] Above all, there is the incongruity that this system of free distribution is seen as gradually evolving from the present state capitalist system in Russia. What is envisaged is a gradual evolution, under the direction of the party, from a form of state capitalism in which workers are paid money wages with which they buy the things they need to a form of state capitalism in which they would be supplied free of charge with the necessities of life, i.e. would in effect be paid entirely in kind.

This perspective of a gradual withering away of commodity production and the money economy was not held

6   It is not impossible that communism will have been established in the socialist countries before the capitalist countries take the socialist path (Mans Dreams, 1966, p. 227). The Party will hold the leading position in communist society for a long time, although its working methods and forms and its structure will naturally alter substantially. The Party, the very embodiment of all that is progressive and organised, will still exist even in the first stages of communism, after its victory on a world scale. It will take communist society many years and even decades before the new mechanisms are fully developed and become maximally effective, before conditions are created for the withering away of the Party. This will be a long and gradual process (ibid., p. 233).

by the CPSU alone but is the general Leninist view of how the so-called transition from socialism to communism will take place. Mandel, for instance, has gone into great detail to show how decommoditization would be economically possible as a series of administrative measures introduced on the basis of state ownership, in response to increases in productivity and inelasticities of market demand (Mandel, 1968, pp. 654-86). Such a gradual transition to full payment in kind is perhaps theoretically conceivable (although in our view highly unlikely), but in any event the end result would not be socialism, since socialism is not payment in kind on the basis of state ownership; nor could socialism be introduced administratively by a state capitalist government.

The definition of communism as state ownership plus payment in kind is shared by nearly all those who have participated in academic debates on so-called pure communism and its feasibility (Wiles, 1962; Sherman, 1970). As a result, most of the discussion which has ensued is irrelevant to socialism/communism considered as a social relationship in which all members of society stand in an equal position with regard to the control of the use of the means of wealth production. We have already seen that a system in which the means of production are owned by a state is not a classless society where all members stand in the same relationship to the means of production, but a class society in which those who control the state stand in a privileged position with regard to the means of production, since they control their use to the exclusion of the rest of society. This is the case even if, as in Leninist theory, this controlling group is to be a vanguard party conceived as being dedicated to serving the interests of the excluded majority. As long as a section of society is excluded from controlling the means of production, a class society exists, no matter how generous or well-meaning the ruling class is considered as being. This is one reason why a gradual evolution from state ownership (state capitalism) to common ownership (socialism) is impossible. Such a gradual evolution from a class society to a classless society is impossible because at some stage there would have to be a rupture which would deprive the state capitalist ruling class be they well-meaning or, more likely, otherwise of their exclusive control over the means of production. There would have to be, in other words, a political and social revolution in which the power to control the use of the means of production would be consciously transferred by the excluded majority from the minority state capitalist class to all members of society.

An equally fundamental reason why a gradual evolution from state capitalism to socialism is impossible is the difference in the form which wealth takes in the two societies. In socialism wealth appears simply in its natural form (as various use values capable of satisfying human wants), while under state capitalism wealth takes the form of value (goods having acquired an exchange value in addition to their natural use value).

As the totality of wealth produced today is a single product produced by the whole workforce acting as a collective labourer (Marx, 1919 (vol. I) pp. 383-4), some goods cannot be produced in the one form and some in the other. The social product that is wealth today can only be produced either wholly as value or wholly as simple use value. Certainly some goods can be directly distributed in kind while others remain obtainable only against payment in money, but this is not the same thing. In this case the goods produced for distribution in kind would still be value in that their production costs, i.e. the exchange value used up in producing them, would have to be paid for out of the surplus value realised in the priced goods sector. Profit-and-loss accounting in units of value would still be necessary. This is why all schemes such as Mandels for a gradual withering away of commodity production insist on the need to retain some universal unit of account (whether this be monetary units as in the various schemes for shadow prices or units of labour-time as an attempt to measure economic value directly) in both the price and the free goods sector.

The changeover from commodity production to production solely for use can only take place as a rupture, not as a gradual transition. Since classless society and common ownership are synonyms, and since commodity production is a nonsense on the basis of common ownership, this rupture (revolution) is in fact the same as the one needed to move from class society to classless society. Neither classes nor the state nor commodity production nor money can gradually wither away. It is no more reasonable to assume that state capitalism could change by degrees into socialism than was the assumption of the classical reformists that private capitalism could be so transformed.

Conclusion

The alternative to capitalism as a society already existing on a world scale is, to define it somewhat negatively, a frontierless, classless, stateless, wageless, moneyless world. Or, more positively:

The new system must be world-wide. *It must be*

a world commonwealth. The world must be regarded as one country and humanity as one people.

All the people will co-operate to produce and distribute all the goods and services which are needed by mankind, each person, willingly and freely, taking part in the way he feels he can do best.

All goods and services will be produced for use only, and having been produced, will be distributed, *free*, directly to the people so that each persons needs are fully satisfied.

The land, factories, machines, mines, roads, railways, ships, and all those things which mankind needs to carry on producing the means of life, will belong to the whole of the people.
(Philoren, 1943 emphases in original)

Opinions may legitimately differ as to whether or not such a society is feasible. That is a separate question. However, in the interests of clarity, we suggest that those who pose as critics of capitalism, but who consider that the society outlined above is not feasible in the immediate future, should refrain from using the term socialism to refer to any society in which money, wages and the state exist. There already exists a perfectly adequate term to refer to such a society capitalism or, as the case may be, state capitalism. It merely confuses the issue to talk of socialism being anything other than a moneyless, wageless, stateless world commonwealth.

The Thin Red Line: Non-Market Socialism in the Twentieth Century

From a socialist standpoint, what is the most crucial difference between the nineteenth century and the twentieth century?

Although one could point to numerous differences which are significant for socialists, surely the most crucial difference of all is that in the nineteenth century there were no states which claimed to be socialist. Despite the well-known distinction which Marx, Engels and others made between 'scientific socialism' and 'utopian socialism', even nineteenth-century 'scientific socialism' was utopian in the etymological sense of referring to nowhere – to no existing state. By way of contrast, for most of the twentieth century, states have existed which have been popularly regarded as 'socialist' or 'communist'. The effect of this popular identification of 'socialism' with certain states has been disastrous. Millions of wage-earners have drawn the conclusion that socialism has been tried in the twentieth century and found to fail. Even many stern critics of the 'socialist states' have been reduced to describing such countries as examples of 'actually existing socialism'.[1] Capitalism has been given a new lease of life because, compared with the brutality of state capitalist regimes or the

1   Rudolph Bahro, *The Alternative in Eastern Europe* (London: New Left Books, 1978).

cynicism of Social Democratic administrations, government by even avowedly capitalist parties has seemed preferable to many.

Social democracy and leninism

During the twentieth century, 'socialism' has come to mean for most people either Social Democracy or Leninism. Social Democracy has been strongest in the countries of Western and Northern Europe, where Social Democratic Parties have held power for varying lengths of time. Most Social Democratic governments have practised a policy of selective nationalisation, bringing key (and often problem-ridden) industries under state control. Implicit in such a policy has been both the preservation of the state, which is obviously strengthened as sectors of the economy are brought under its control, and the preservation of capitalism. Social Democracy has had the effect of preserving capitalism because the Social Democratic 'mixed economy' is a mixture of private capitalism and state capitalism. Private companies in the 'mixed economy' remain profit-making enterprises. Part of their profits is reinvested in production, while the residue is partly consumed by capitalists who own shares in the companies and partly acquired by the state in the form of taxes. The nationalised sectors of the 'mixed economy' conform to this pattern of profit distribution no less than private companies. State enterprises are intended to make profits, although lack of commercial viability has often been a reason for declining industries being nationalised. Where profits are realised by nationalised concerns, there is the same three-way division of the profits as in private industry, between the reinvestment fund, the state, and capitalists who own shares or bonds.

Throughout the 'mixed economy', in private and nationalised concerns alike, goods and services are produced for sale on the market. Production is geared to market requirements rather than to human needs, and distribution of goods and services is handled by buying and selling operations, achieved by the use of money. Similarly, throughout the 'mixed economy', production is undertaken by working men and women who sell their labour power for wages (or salaries). Whether the 'mixed economy' is considered from the viewpoint of consumers, whose level of consumption is determined by the money at their disposal, or from the viewpoint of wage-earners, who must sell their labour power to an enterprise which is prepared to employ them, the differences between the private capitalist and state capitalist sectors of the economy are insignificant.[2]

At its most well-meaning, Social Democracy has represented an attempt to humanise and reform capitalism by means of state intervention. One reason why Social Democrats have failed in their attempts to transform capitalism into a humane system is that invariably they have attempted to carry out their reforms within the narrow confines of a single nation- state, which has necessarily remained an integral part of the world market. In the end, the world market has had a more decisive influence on the production of wealth and the intensity of labour than the however-well-intentioned reforms legislated by Social Democrats. Social Democrats inevitably have been driven to administer capitalism in the only way it can be administered – against the

2   Adam Buick and John Crump, *State Capitalism: the Wages System under New Management* (London: Macmillan, 1986).

interests of the wage-earning majority. Social Democracy has suffered this fate of continuing to oppress
wage-earners not because of the failure of its leaders,
because they lacked will and nerve, but because of the
very nature of capitalism. Nevertheless, it is fair to say
that once most Social Democrats have tasted state
power, and have found themselves responding to the
dictates of the world market, so their good intentions
have rapidly been eroded by political cynicism. The
record of Social Democracy in the twentieth century has
not only been one of submission to capitalism, but also
one of support for wars, apology for privilege and com-
promise with the spurious democracy of parliamentar-
ism. The result of advocating a 'mixed economy' is that
the achievement of 'socialism' has been endlessly post-
poned. The Social Democrats' 'socialism' continually
has receded into the future, in a similar fashion, as we
shall see, to the 'communism' of the Leninists.

In contrast to Social Democracy, most of the
countries where Leninist Parties have taken power have
been located in Eastern Europe and East Asia. The different geographical locations of Social Democracy and
Leninism reflect the fact that these two political move-
ments have developed in response to the needs of
countries at different stages of economic development.
Whereas Social Democracy has made little headway in
other than advanced countries, Leninism has largely
been confined to backward countries. Except in the
case of certain East European countries, where the
imposition of the Leninist political model has resulted
from the extension of Russian military influence, Leninist Parties have generally captured power against a back-

cloth of revolutionary upheaval arising from the failure of the pre-revolutionary regimes to achieve sustained economic growth and industrialisation.

Following the revolutionary seizure of power, Leninism proceeds with an attempt to achieve forced economic development by means of restricting workers' and peasants' consumption in the interest of rapid capital accumulation. Under these circumstances, in Leninist vocabulary, 'socialism' means a policy of generalised nationalisation (at least within the industrial sectors of the economy) and a vast increase in wage labour, since newly created enterprises require fresh drafts of wage-earners to operate them. The strengthening of the state by virtue of its role as the general employer, and the extension of wage labour, clearly contradict the nineteenth-century socialist prescriptions that the state should wither away and that the wages system should be abolished. Leninism has 'solved' this problem ideologically by relegating the withering away of the state and the abolition of wages to a continually receding 'communist' future. Meanwhile, the term 'socialism' is retained as a descriptive label for a situation where the state has unparalleled power and where workers have no alternative but to work for wages in order to gain the means of life. In other words, Leninism uses a 'socialist' label to hide the real nature of an economy which differs from private capitalism only in the fact that the state has replaced the privately owning capitalist class as the owner of the means of production. Since the countries where Leninist Parties hold power exhibit all the key features of capitalism (production for profit, monetary distribution, wage labour, accumulation of capital) and are forced to attune their production in line with international competition as it registers on the world market, they are best understood as state capitalist countries. Ibid. [3]

If state capitalism expresses the *economic* reality of Leninism, *politically* the hallmark of Leninism is the extreme concentration of power. No political formation is tolerated outside the umbrella of the ruling triumvirate, made up of the party, the state and the armed forces. The vanguard party operates in the name of the working class but in fact looks after the interests of the *de facto* state capitalist class, which is composed of the upper echelons of the party, state and military hierarchies. Nationalism and militarism are other important ingredients in the political cocktail of Leninism, and the prominent role which they play reflects the economic backwardness of most countries where Leninist Parties have taken power. In the cut-throat world of capitalist competition, economic backwardness is generally accompanied by subordination to imperialism, so that revolutions aimed at developing a backward country on a state capitalist basis are also expressions of national independence. Hence, flying in the face of. the socialist common sense of the nineteenth century that 'the working men have no country',[44] Leninist Parties that have come to power have attempted to hitch the working class to the chariot of military defence of national interests.

3   Ibid.

4   Karl Marx and Frederick Engels, *Collected Works*, vol. VI (London: Lawrence & Wishart, 1976) p. 502.

For the reasons outlined above, our contention is that Social Democracy and Leninism are bankrupt insofar as the interests of the wage-earning working class are concerned. Anyone who has preserved the critical consciousness of nineteenth century non-market socialism can see that, in the twentieth century, Social Democracy and Leninism have bolstered, rather than subverted, capitalism. The bankruptcy of Social Democracy and Leninism should be particularly clear in the light of the present economic crisis. The crisis has arisen because the chaotic nature of capitalism has led to capital's inability to realise sufficient profit in production, and hence to a contracting world market. It has been a worldwide crisis, affecting private capitalist, 'mixed economy' and state capitalist countries alike. Social Democracy and Leninism have been unable to offer any credible solutions to the crisis (and are unable to solve the hardships which capitalism imposes on wage-earners even outside of crisis situations) because the alternatives to private capitalism which they represent are no more than alternative methods of organising capitalism. They have no alternative to production for the world market, even though it is the world market which has produced the crisis.

The thin red line

To find a coherent set of ideas which are subversive of capitalism, and which do offer an alternative to production for the world market, one must turn to the 'thin red line' represented by the five currents which are examined in the following chapters. In roughly chronological order of appearance, these five currents are: anarcho-communism; impossibilism; council communism; Bordigism; situationism. A thorough consideration of each current will be left until the relevant chapter, but there are brief profiles of these currents in the Introduction for the benefit of readers who may be unfamiliar with them.

Even a perfunctory acquaintance with the five currents which jointly represent the 'thin red line' of non-market socialism in the twentieth century leads to the realisation that their importance does not lie in the number of their adherents, or in their influence on the course of world history. Although some of these currents have enjoyed moments of transitory glory/notoriety, throughout most of the twentieth century it has been possible to discount them in terms of the support which they have attracted and their impact on the world. The question therefore arises: if the significance of the non-market socialists does not lie in their numbers and influence, where does it lie? The answer is that non-market socialism is significant because its various currents represent successful attempts by groups of working men and women to formulate a fundamental critique of capitalism and simultaneously to pose a genuinely socialist alternative. Considered in isolation, it is easy to dismiss anyone of the five currents as too small and too uninfluential to be important. Taken together, however, they represent a sustained response on the part of wage labour to capitalist exploitation and irrationality. Irrespective of the limited numbers of wage-earners involved, non-market socialism should be seen as an authentic response to capitalism by wage labour because, as the existence of the various non-market socialist currents demonstrates, groups of wage-earners have repeatedly, and largely independently of one another, formulated the same critique of capitalism and the same alternative of socialism. The fact that this has occurred at different historical junctures, and in different geographical and cultural contexts, gives weight to the claim that, as long as world capitalism persists, groups of wage-earning men and women are certain to emerge who will challenge capital's priority of production for the market and call on their fellow-workers to take joint action in order to establish the human community of socialism.

It is important to emphasise the scale of the claim which is being made here with regard to non-market socialism. It is not being suggested that non-market socialism is another socialist tradition which should be placed alongside Social Democracy and Leninism, and seen as a rival to them. The claim is considerably more audacious than that. What is being argued is that, collectively, anarcho-communism, impossibilism, council communism, Bordigism and situationism *are* socialism in the twentieth century. Outside these currents, socialism has not existed, since what conventionally are considered to be the great victories of 'socialism' in the twentieth century have been nothing more than extensions of state capitalism at the expense of private capitalism. Social Democracy and Leninism have made priceless contributions to world capitalism by deflecting working-class criticism away from the key elements of capitalism as a mode of production to the contingent, and increasingly obsolete, manifestations of capitalism in its private capitalist form. Only those working men and women who have looked at capitalism from the perspective provided by non-market socialism have been able to see through capitalism in all its forms and have avoided capitulation to one side or another in struggles between rival capitalist interests.

Implicit in this argument is a criticism of the conventional method of political analysis, which seeks to understand the world in terms of a 'left'/'right' dichotomy. The 'left' and the 'right' are different only to the extent that they provide a different political and organisational apparatus for administering the same capitalist system. What the 'left' and the 'right' have in common is that they both accept the world market is the framework in which they must operate. Since both the 'left' and the 'right' stand for the perpetuation of wage labour, it follows that they cannot offer convincing solutions to the problems which inevitably confront wage-earners. A permanent solution to the problems which are inherent in wage labour, such as insecurity and intensity of work, can only lie in the abolition of the wages system. Yet the abolition of the wages system is a demand which cannot be located on the 'left'-'right' political spectrum. Only the various currents which represent non-market socialism have consistently demanded an end to wage labour, and that is why they too cannot usefully be identified in terms of a 'left'/'right' orientation.

The principles of socialism

In order to sustain the claim that, collectively, anarchocommunism, impossibilism, council communism, Bordigism and situationism are twentieth-century socialism, it needs to demonstrated that there is a basic set of socialist principles which these currents share. Initially, four such principles can be identified. The currents of non-market socialism are all committed to establishing a new society where:

1. Production will be for use, and not for sale on

the market.

2. Distribution will be according to need, and not by means of buying and selling.

3. Labour will be voluntary, and not imposed on workers by means of a coercive wages system.

4. A human community will exist, and social divisions based on class, nationality, sex or race will have disappeared.

Let us clarify these four principles for those readers who may not immediately grasp all their ramifications.

1. Production for use

The means of production will be owned and controlled communally, and will be used to produce whatever men, women and children need to enjoy full and satisfying lives. Levels of production will be determined by people's freely expressed desires – that is, their desires for articles of individual and social consumption and their desires to engage in creative work. Communal ownership means that all people will freely have access to the means of production, and that no section of the population will be able to exclude others from using the means of production or from enjoying the fruits of production. Production will be coordinated at local, regional and global levels, and communal control means that all people will again be free to participate in managing production and administering society as a whole. Just as no individual or group will be able to prevent others from engaging in direct production, so no section of the population will be able to exclude others from the management of production or from the administration of society.

The details of what to produce and how to produce

will be decided locally. The responsibilities of the regional and global bodies will be threefold. In the first place, they will provide the statistical services which will allow production to be coordinated. Second, they will ensure that products which localities need but cannot produce are available to those localities. Third, they will handle the movement of local products at the regional and global levels. By confining the functions of regional and global bodies to these activities, they will not assume the role which the state fulfils in class-divided societies. They will not be provided with armed forces, and therefore will not be in a position to impose decisions on others.

All this is in evident contrast to capitalism. Like any mode of production, capitalism is provided with a mechanism for coordinating production. In capitalism's case, this mechanism is the market. But the price inherent in relying on the market IS that levels of production are determined not by people's social or even biological needs, but by the population's 'effective demand' expressed as buying power. The needs of those without the ability to pay do not register on the market, and this results in means of production lying idle while millions of people are deprived. Such a barbaric situation would be Impossible in the society envisaged by non-market socialists.

2. Distribution according to need

People will be free to take whatever they choose from the consumption outlets ('shops without cash registers') in the new society, without making any payment, since money will not exist. Similarly, people will freely make use of social facilities, such as theatres and libraries, without entering into exchange relationships (i.e. buying tickets or paying fees). Non-market socialists are confident that society could run, smoothly on this basis, without being undermined by people becoming insatiably greedy or indulging in recklessly extravagant consumption. Our confidence derives from a number of considerations. First, the production of useful articles would be much greater in the new society than in capitalism, not only because production would be freed from the constraints of the market, but also because all those presently engaged in activities which are specific to a commercial society (banking, insurance and so on), or in activities which are specific to a class-divided society (such as staffing the numerous arms of the repressive apparatus of the state), could redirect their efforts towards production. Second, since greed and conspicuous consumption are reactions to scarcity, we can expect these forms of behaviour to disappear in a society which raises production to the level where it guarantees everyone an abundant supply of all that is required for a comfortable and satisfying life. Third, in a society which is based on cooperation rather than competition, not only would the individual's sense of solidarity induce him or her to exercise self-control on occasions when this was necessary, but social disapproval would be a powerful restraint on any who were disposed to reckless extravagance.

3. Voluntary labour

In the new society, everyone will have the right to consume, irrespective of whether they are engaged in productive activity or not. Nevertheless, non-market socialists anticipate that people will volunteer to work, and will freely give their time and effort to ensure that an abundant supply of products is constantly available. To those whose horizons do not extend beyond capitalist society, these expectations must seem preposterous. Under capitalism, workers are coerced into engaging in production by the system which makes their consumption dependent on their wages. Work within capitalism therefore is conflated with employment, and popularly is regarded merely as a means to leisure (= consumption), which becomes the end to which life is supposed to be directed.

However, non-market socialists argue that once work and employment are conceptually distinguished, work can be seen as an activity which is not merely enjoyable, but which it is biologically necessary for human beings to engage in (on a par with eating, drinking, breathing and sex). Freed from its alienating form of wage labour, work will become a creative and rewarding experience which it would be painful for people to deprive themselves of. The boring and monotonous toil of capitalism will be replaced by stimulating and diversified patterns of work, and many of the dangerous occupations which are found within capitalism will be eliminated.

Capitalism has already made these changes technically possible, but is prevented from realising them because considerations of profit outweigh human welfare. Any dangerous work which remains in the new society will be undertaken voluntarily and the only reward for the men and women engaged in it will be society's affection and esteem (as with lifeboat crews and mountain rescue teams, for example, even under capitalism).

4. A human community

Capitalism is a divided society. The basic divisions within capitalism are class divisions, which exist because the means of production are owned and controlled by sections of the population and not by society as a whole. Sectional ownership can be maintained only when it is constantly reinforced by the state, and since states exercise their authority over geographical areas, national divisions are perpetuated by capitalism. Furthermore, since labour power is a marketable commodity under capitalism, wage-earners throughout the world compete with one another to sell their labour power to those who employ them. Such competition forms the basis of the sexual, racial and other divisions which divide the working class, and which are skilfully manipulated by the ruling class in order to maintain capital's ascendancy over wage labour.

The society envisaged by non-market socialists would remove all these divisions at one stroke, by realising the communal ownership of the means of production. Since capitalism is an integrated economic system whose market encompasses the whole world, it can be removed only by an equally world-enveloping system which displaces the market.

The new society which non-market socialists envisage must therefore be a human community on a global scale. National frontiers will not exist. Cultural and linguistic diversity might flourish within the human community of socialism, but in a moneyless world where distribution was according to need, there would be no way in which the embracing of a certain culture or the use of a certain language could confer economic advantages or disadvantages. In a world owned by all, all would be brothers and sisters.

Although these four basic socialist principles are shared by the currents which represent non-market socialism, they are not sufficient for distinguishing the non-market socialists from all their political opponents. We said before that 'communism' figures in Leninist ideology as a mirage which is forever receding into the distance, and this enables Leninists of all hues to sub-scribe *in the long term* to these four basic socialist prin-ciples. For example, books published with the approval of the Russian state inform us that:

> Under communism, consumer goods – to say nothing of capital goods [sic] – cease to be com-modities. Trade and money will outlive them-selves. Flats, cultural, communication and trans-port facilities, meals, laundries, clothes, etc., will all be free.
>
> Stores and shops will be turned into public warehouses where members of communist soci-ety will be supplied with commodities [sic] for personal use. The need for wages and other forms of remuneration will disappear.[5]

Apart from the silly slips about capital and commodities existing in communism, this could be taken as an accept-able sketch of the new society. Even better – since he drops Lenin's arbitrary distinction between 'socialism' and 'communism' – is what the Trotskyist Ernest Mandel has written about a 'socialist economy':

> The withering-away of commodity and money economy is, however, only one of the factors bringing about the disappearance of social inequality, classes and the state.[6]

5   *Man's Dreams Are Coming True* (Moscow: Progress, 1966) p. 224.

A fifth principle is therefore required in order to distinguish the non-market socialists from all varieties of Leninists, including the Trotskyists. This principle can be formulated as follows:

5. Opposition to capitalism as it manifests itself in *all* existing countries.

Non-market socialists do not take sides in the wars and struggles for supremacy between rival states which are a permanent feature of world capitalism. On the contrary, non-market socialists are hostile to all states, including those which falsely proclaim themselves as 'socialist' or 'workers' states'. Indeed, it was the various currents of non-market socialists who pioneered the theory of state capitalism in order to clarify the nature of self-styled 'workers' states', starting with Russia, and in order to give a theoretical explanation for their refusal to support such states.

State capitalism

Following the Russian Revolution of 1917, the US government deported a number of activists who were of Russian origin, including the anarcho-communists Alexander Berkman and Emma Goldman. Berkman and Goldman went to Russia and observed Leninist rule at first hand. On the basis of his experiences, Berkman described the Russian economy in 1922 as 'a combination of State and private capitalism'[7] and this view was

---

6   Ernest Mandel, *Marxist Economic Theory* (London: Merlin, 1968) p.673.

7   Alexander Berkman, *The Russian Tragedy* (Sanday: Cienfuegos, 1976) p.25.

echoed by anarcho-communists elsewhere. As Osugi Sakae wrote in Japan, also in 1922: 'the struggle between the proletariat on one side and state and private capitalism on the other is still continuing in Russia'.[8]

The council communist Otto Ruhle journeyed to Russia in 1920 and reported in 1921, after his return to Germany, that: 'The dictatorship of the party is commissar-despotism, is state capitalism.'[9] A decade later, various council communist groups issued in Holland a set of *Theses on Bolshevism,* which declared in part:

> The socialization concept of the Bolsheviks is therefore nothing but a capitalist economy taken over by the State and directed from the outside and above by its bureaucracy. The Bolshevik socialism is state-organized capitalism.[10]

Despite the fact that no members of the impossibilist Socialist Party of Great Britain (SPGB) visited Russia in the Immediate aftermath of the 1917 Revolution, by 1920 from its vantage point in Britain, the *Socialist Standard* was already able to discern that Leninist policy amounted to state capitalism.[11] At a later stage, when Lenin was dead and his successors were engaged in a

8   Osugi Sakae, 'Rono Roshia no Shin Rodo Undo', in *Osugi Sakae Zenshu*, vol. II (Tokyo: 1963) p. 604.

9   Otto Rühle, *From the Bourgeois to the Proletarian Revolution* (London and Glasgow: Socialist Reproduction/Revolutionary Perspectives, 1974) p. xvii.

10   *The Bourgeois Role of Bolshevism* (Glasgow: Glasgow People's Press, no date) p. 21.

11   *Socialist Standard*, July 1920.

vicious struggle for power, the SPGB clearly expressed the non-market socialist conviction that, since Leninists of all types are advocates of capitalism, from a working-class standpoint there is nothing to choose between them. Commenting on the struggle between Stalin and Trotsky, the *Socialist Standard* wrote: 'Both Trotsky and Stalin draw up their programmes within the framework of state and private capitalism which prevails in Russia.'[12]

Although the Bordigists and the situationists reached the conclusion that state capitalism exists in Russia and elsewhere at a later stage than the other currents of non-market socialists, for many years now all five currents have attempted to dispel popular illusions about the state capitalist countries. Not only have they exposed the capitalist features of the state capitalist countries, but they have counterposed to state capitalism the alternative vision of a genuinely socialist society which could liberate humankind from indignity and oppression by incorporating principles 1-4 which we outlined above. It is this, above all, which distinguishes the non-market socialists from the Trotskyists and other varieties of Leninists. The Trotskyists have been inhibited from counterposing to capitalism the alternative of non-market socialism, because the focus of their attention has been the relatively minor differences which exist between traditional, private capitalism and capitalism as it manifests itself in their so-called 'workers' states'. To express this schematically, the Trotskyists' failure to embrace principle 5 has caused principles 1-4 to be relegated to (at best) the background of their concerns. Alternatively, one could say that the Trotskyists have lost their

---

12   *Socialist Standard*, December 1928.

'utopianism' (i.e. their identification with no nation-state) by allowing themselves to be sucked into struggles between rival capitals and by electing to defend some capitalist states against others. This has resulted in an unbridgeable divide between Trotskyism and the five currents of non-market socialism.

Differences between the non-market socialists

Having identified the five principles which the various currents of non-market socialists collectively hold, the issues which have separated these currents and provoked their mutual criticism must also be considered briefly.

The anarcho-communists have seen Marxism as yet another form of politics which seeks to maintain the power of the state. Not only have anarcho-communists identified Marxism with statism in general, but in particular they have identified Marxism with the Leninist states. They have argued that the characteristics of Leninist state capitalism derive from the Marxist principles on which it claims to be based. Conversely, just as the anarcho-communists generally have made no distinction between Marxism and Leninism, so the other non-market socialist currents have reciprocated by indiscriminately lumping the anarcho-communists together with all other varieties of anarchists, be they Stirnerite individualists, anarcho-capitalist 'libertarians' or whatever. In other words, they have chosen to ignore the commitment of the anarcho-communists to communism.

Although not all impossibilists have been committed to parliamentary activity, the SPGB – as the best-known impossibilist group – has been separated from the other currents of non-market socialists perhaps above all by its belief that parliamentary elections can be put to a revolutionary use. The SPGB has insisted that the paradigm of socialist revolution consists of the working class consciously electing a majority of socialist MPs to the national assemblies in different countries, whereupon 'the machinery of government ... may be converted from an instrument of oppression into the agent of emancipation'.[13] A parliamentary strategy of this type has been anathema to the other currents of non-market socialists.

Council communism has emphasised the part to be played by councils in the projected socialist revolution, and has combined its advocacy of councils with hostility towards trade unions. One repercussion of this emphasis on councils has been a perennial difficulty faced by council communists when it comes to deciding the respective roles of the workers' councils and the political party. Hence, one can say that not only has the council communists' emphasis on councils separated them from the other currents of non-market socialists, but that it has also acted as a source of division among the council communists themselves. In extreme cases, attachment to the workers' councils as an organisational form has entirely eclipsed the communist element in council communism, resulting in a variety of 'councilism' which is compatible with production for the market.

The Bordigists have seen themselves as a vanguard which must lead the working class to socialism. Their conviction that they have the responsibility to lead the working class derives from the premise that only after the achievement of socialism could the mass of the workers become conscious socialists. The other currents of non-market socialists have denounced the Bordigists' vanguard-

13 SPGB, *Declaration of Principles* (1904).

ism and have argued that (to quote from the statutes of the First International) 'the emancipation of the working class must be the act of the working class itself'[14] and not of self-appointed leaders.

Perhaps because of their artistic origins, the situationists have often seemed to be more concerned with self-expression than with communicating their ideas to wage-earners. The situationists have seen the other currents of non-market socialists as outdated and, at best, the products of earlier stages of capitalist development. On the other hand, the other currents of non-market socialists have often criticised the situationists as 'modernists' who have been overly influenced by current intellectual fashions and who have shirked the arduous toil of sustained, organised activity within the working class.

The differences between the various currents of non-market socialists are deep-rooted and have acted to keep these currents separate from one another and mutually hostile. Despite this, the claim which is advanced here is that these differences constitute a 'periphery' which is relatively less important than the commonly held 'core' of socialist principles which were examined earlier. What grounds are there for regarding the 'core' as more significant than the 'periphery'? Essentially, the argument is that the 'core' principles of socialism relate to the vital task of posing a socialist alternative to capitalism, while the 'peripheral' differences largely arise from the debate over how socialism can be achieved (by means of parliamentary elections, workers' councils, vanguard parties and so on). Of course, one cannot pretend that the method of achiev-

14   David Fernbach, *Karl Marx: the Revolutions of 1848 – Political Writings*, vol. I (Harmondsworth: Penguin, 1973) p. 65.

ing socialism is an unimportant question. Certainly, the choice of means has implications for the nature of the projected end. Nevertheless, in the circumstances of the twentieth century, when socialism is widely misunderstood as Social Democracy and Leninism, the prime responsibility of socialists is to encourage wage-earners, as they come into conflict with capital, to see that a non-market alternative to capitalist production represents the only lasting solution to their problems. In this regard, all five currents of non-market socialists have played a positive role. On the other hand, precisely because for most of this century mere handfuls of wage-earners have been committed to non-market socialism, the fierce polemics over the means to achieve socialism which non-market socialists have engaged in have been largely academic.

One can illustrate the above argument by taking the Bordigists as an example and considering further their commitment to vanguardism. As has already been mentioned, with the exception of the Bordigists, most non-market socialists reject the idea that a vanguard can lead the wage-earners to socialism. They interpret the maxim of the First International that 'the emancipation of the working class must be the act of the working class itself' to mean that capitalism can only be overthrown, and that socialism can only be achieved, by a majority of conscious socialists. On the other hand, the Bordigists believe that a socialist majority is unattainable under capitalism. They envisage the socialist revolution in terms of action by a vanguard because they insist that only in the changed material conditions of socialism could the majority become socialists.

Some non-market socialists would see this as suffi-

cient reason for denying that the Bordigists are socialists. However, I think it can be shown that the Bordigists' vanguardism is not crucially important in the
present situation. Like the other currents of non-market
socialists, the Bordigists engage in activity to challenge
capitalist ideology and to popularise socialist ideas.
Depending on the country and the cultural environment
in which they exist, wage-earners may stumble across
the Bordigists or across one of the other currents of
non-market socialism. Just as with any other current of
non-market socialism, wage-earners who make contact
with the Bordigists will find the experience useful for
gaining a recognition of what socialism genuinely
means. Similarly, they can gain from the Bordigists an
understanding that capitalism is a single, unified world
system, which exists in all countries and dominates the
entire globe. Looked at in this way, the question of vanguardism has little significance *under present circumstances.*
Any wage-earner who encounters the Bordigists and is
impressed by their theories is accepted as part of the vanguard. Nobody who agrees is turned away; it is assumed
that they are part of the vanguard.

The Bordigists' image of themselves as a vanguard is
not vitally important at present because the question of
vanguardism will ultimately be settled by the practical
actions of wage-earners at the relevant time. It is up to the
wage-earners to carry out the socialist revolution and to
prove the Bordigists wrong. Of course, if the Bordigists
persisted with their determination to act as a vanguard
even in the face of a majority of conscious socialists, the
situation would be drastically different from that which
currently pertains – and this would call for a drastically dif-

ferent response. Suppose that under the circumstances where a majority of conscious socialists were actually engaged in transforming society to socialism, the Bordigists were to proclaim: 'Hands off the socialist revolution! It is our affair. We do not recognise that you workers are capable of achieving socialist consciousness.' Clearly, in such a situation, additional principles to those which have been formulated to cover *present* circumstances would swiftly be generated, and equally swiftly (and deservedly) the workers would sweep the Bordigists and all other would-be leaders aside.

Implicit in the foregoing discussion is the idea that the distinction between 'core' and 'periphery' is not fixed, but reflects the prevailing circumstances. In the current situation, the prime responsibility of socialists is to challenge the economic mechanism and the set of social relations which constitute capitalism by demonstrating that society would be organised differently in socialism. The core principles of socialism which were formulated earlier are a reflection of this priority, in that they are principally concerned with the question of (capitalist or socialist) ends. In a different situation, when the socialist revolution was imminent, the question of means (how to effect the socialist transformation of society) would also demand urgent attention. Consequently, the key principles of socialism would necessarily have to be extended in order to encompass the pressing questions of means as well as ends. As a result, the boundary between 'core' and 'peripheral' questions would naturally alter, and a more extensive set of criteria for distinguishing socialists from non-socialists would be required than at present. However, to anticipate this development, and to construct artificially an extended set of socialist principles which encompass means as well as ends, even when the circumstances of the socialist revolution lie in the future and hence are speculative, is to ignore material conditions and to construct a suprahistorical theory.

One reason why the distinction between 'core' and 'peripheral' areas of their theory has not been made by the non-market socialists is the tendency of most currents to set themselves up as a minuscule group or 'party', which boasts a detailed programme encompassing every aspect of socialist theory. Under current conditions, the group then becomes a besieged citadel which confronts not only the hostile capitalist world but also the majority of wage-earners, whose ideas, about socialism are the result of the illusions spread by Social democrats and Leninists. In such a situation, the group battles to maintain its doctrinal purity in the face of the constant threat of being swamped by the ideology of capitalism. The very survival of the group seems to depend on the grim defence of every dot and comma of group doctrine, and the I resulting 'besieged citadel' mentality makes it difficult to distinguish what is crucial in the group's programme from what is contingent (in the terms of this discussion, the 'core' from the 'periphery').

Rejection of the 'transitional society'

If and when the time comes when the mass of wage-earners turn to non-market socialism as the means to liberate themselves, it is possible, and even likely, that all the existing currents of non-market socialists will be superseded and that an entirely new movement will be built. Even so, the 'core' principles of socialism which

the five currents of non-market socialists have collectively maintained will be the theoretical foundation
stones on which a mass movement of genuine socialists
will be constructed. In fact, the process of superseding
the five currents does not lie entirely in the future. It is a
process which proceeds continually, so that in recent
decades new developments have taken place and
groups have emerged which are significant.

In my view, the most important development which
needs to take place within the milieu of non-market socialism (and which, to an extent, is taking place) is for the
notion of a supposed 'transitional society' between capitalism and socialism to be rejected. To the extent that this
development occurs, it enables non-market socialism to
differentiate itself even more clearly from Social Democracy and Leninism, by adding a further principle to the
five socialist principles which we identified earlier. The
sixth principle can be formulated as follows:

6. Capitalism can be transcended only by immediately being replaced by socialism.

To talk in terms of capitalism 'immediately being replaced
by socialism' is not to suggest that socialism will be free of
problems when it is first established. No doubt, the mess
which capitalism has made of the world will ensure that
there are major problems which a newly emergent socialist
society will have to solve. Yet what the phrase 'immediately being replaced by socialism' does imply is that the
solution of these problems bequeathed by capitalism will
have to take place from the outset on a socialist basis.
Various approaches which are popularly misunderstood as
'transitional' can be ruled out in advance. For example, one
could not have bits of socialism transplanted into still-

functioning capitalism, any more than elements of capitalism could be left *in situ* within newly established socialism. Still less could one legitimately describe the doomed offspring which would result from such far-fetched attempts at social hybridisation as a 'transitional society'.

One feature which capitalism and socialism have in common is their all-or-nothing quality, their inability to coexist in today's highly integrated world, which can provide an environment for only one or other of these rival global systems. In the circumstances of the twentieth century, the means of production must either function as capital throughout the world (in which case wage labour and capitalism persist internationally) or they must be commonly owned and democratically controlled at a global level (in which case they would be used to produce wealth for free, worldwide distribution). No halfway house between these two starkly opposed alternatives exists, and it is the impossibility of discovering any viable 'transitional' structures which ensures that the changeover from world capitalism to world socialism will have to take the form of a short, sharp rupture (a revolution), rather than an extended process of cumulative transformation.

How, then, might a newly emergent socialist society solve problems, such as shortage of food, which capitalism has created? The first point to make is that the problem of twentieth-century hunger is a social problem and not a technical problem. Technically, the means to feed the world's population are within humankind's reach, but it is capitalism's priority of production for profit which prevents plentiful conditions from being actually realised. Socialism will remove the straitjacket which calculations of profitability impose on production, so that a situation of abundance – where men, women and children throughout the world will be able to take according to their self-determined needs – will be rapidly achieved.

Nevertheless, accessible though such a situation is, its achievement will require time. The time involved will certainly be nothing like the relatively lengthy process which Marx envisaged in 1875 before 'all the springs of co-operative wealth flow more abundantly'.[15] Nothing is more ridiculous today than to repeat the stale formulae of more than one hundred years ago, and hence to ignore the immense developments in the techniques of producing wealth which capitalism has (or, more accurately, the wage-earning wealth producers within capitalism have) brought about. As far as the production of food is concerned, we are talking of at most a few harvests before enough food – and more than enough – could be produced for every man, woman and child to have free access to whatever they required. How might socialist society organise itself during the intervening months or, at most, few years before actual plenty would be produced?

Certainly the answer is not by constructing a 'transitional society' sandwiched between capitalism and socialism. What will be required will be temporary measures which are compatible with, and will lend strength to, emergent socialism; not the construction of a so-called 'transitional society' which would need to be dismantled before socialism could even be instituted. Obviously, the men and women who have newly established socialism will first turn to the 'milk lakes' and the

15   Karl Marx and Frederick Engels, *Selected Works*, vol. III (Moscow: Progress, 1970) p. 19.

'butter mountains' which capitalism has accumulated because of its inability to sell such commodities profitably on the world markets. Many nation-states also have strategic stocks of vital supplies, designed to provide some security against the disruption of supplies in the event of war. Since the establishment of socialism will entail the immediate abolition of all markets, nations and wars, sources of supply such as these will be turned to socially useful ends and made freely available.

The scale of any shortages which could not be eliminated by such stop-gap measures is a matter of speculation, but let us assume that shortages would exist for a time before production on a socialist basis could get fully under way and abundance could be attained. How would socialist men and women handle such shortages? It is out of the question that they would make selective use of the wages system or monetary distribution. Such measures would not be 'transitional' but would instead guarantee the continuation of capitalism. Equally unthinkable would be any suggestion that a machinery of state might be retained temporarily as a 'transitional' apparatus for enforcing a rationing system. The persistence of the state would signify that class divisions had not been eradicated. Newly emergent socialism, struggling to solve the problems which it has inherited from capitalism, will have to meet any shortages by relying on the very item it can safely be assumed it will have in abundance: revolutionary enthusiasm.

In the *Critique of the Gotha Programme,* Marx asserted that 'Right can never be higher than the economic structure of society and its cultural development condi-

tioned thereby.'[16] With regard to the long-term functioning of socialist society, he was absolutely right. Any
attempt to run socialism, year after year, by compensating for material shortages by ideological appeals to
revolutionary enthusiasm would be bound to fail. But
thanks to the material advances brought about by capitalism, long-term shortages are not the problems with
which socialism would now have to grapple. The problems which are likely to arise are those associated with
temporary shortfalls prior to the attainment of abundance; and it is precisely such a transient situation which
could be negotiated by relying on revolutionary solidarity.

It will be the revolutionary enthusiasm of millions of
socialist men and women, and their determination to make
a success of the new society, which will bring about the
transformation of the capitalist world in the first place, as
they take whatever actions are necessary to bring the
means of production under common ownership. These
same qualities of enthusiasm and determination will not
suddenly evaporate as soon as the means of production are
freed from their role of capital. They will exist as a massive
reservoir of popular commitment to the goals of socialism,
and it is these reserves of revolutionary ardour which
people will be able to tap in order to tide society over any
period of temporary scarcity. It will be no great hardship
for revolutionary men and women to restrict voluntarily
certain areas of their own consumption until universal
plenty is secured. Having recently stormed the citadels of
capitalist power, these selfsame revolutionary men and
women will make light of any further period of temporary

16   Ibid, p.19.

and selective self-restraint that is necessary – perceiving it as a continuation of the revolution, a small additional price to pay in order to eliminate capitalist misery and indignity for ever.

It always was an illusion to imagine that the route from capitalist scarcity to socialist abundance lies along a diversionary path marked with signposts to an imaginary 'transitional society'. The route to socialism has to be direct; as a moneyless, classless, stateless world community, socialism has to be achieved immediately, or not at all; and any temporary lack of abundance has to be compensated for by the revolutionary enthusiasm of the millions of men and women who will be the collective builders of the socialist world. Fortunately, it is the technological advances of capitalism which have ensured that – given the will for socialism – full-scale abundance can be instituted rapidly. In the light of the productive potential now available to humankind, the notion of a 'transitional society' should clearly be seen not as a bridge leading beyond 'capitalism, but rather as an ideological barrier obstructing the path to socialism.

The idea of a society which acts as a 'transitional' stage between capitalism and socialism has largely been absent from the thinking of the anarcho-communists, impossibilists and situationists, but it has been entertained by some council communists and the Bordigists. For example, in 1930 the Group of International Communists of Holland (GIC) borrowed some of Marx's speculations in the *Critique of the Gotha Programme* and envisaged a 'transitional society' based on exchange and labour-time calculation.[17] As for the Bordigists,

17 'Temps de travail social moyen: base d'une production et d'une repartition communiste', Supplement to *Informations Correspondances*

they have taken the view that the party should exercise power after the revolution and administer a society which essentially would remain capitalist for a period until socialism could be achieved. We have seen the dire effects which result from the Trotskyist belief that Russia, China and the other state capitalist countries are 'transitional' 'workers' states'. Council communist and Bordigist ideas have been less damaging because, unlike the Trotskyists, these currents do not identify their notional 'transitional society' with any existing state. Yet, even so, all notions of a 'transitional society' are both mistaken and fraught with peril. They are mistaken because capitalism and socialism (as market and non-market societies respectively) are totally incompatible, so that no 'transitional' combination of capitalist and socialist elements is possible. They are perilous because entertaining the notion of a 'transitional society' inevitably results in the goal of socialism, to a greater or lesser extent, being eclipsed. It is for these reasons that I have argued that all non-market socialists should reject the notion that a 'transitional society' will be interposed between capitalism and socialism. The problems confronting humankind are too grim to allow the wage-earners of the world to solve them by 'transitional' half measures. Only the complete abolition of the market, classes, the state and national frontiers offers hope for the future.

Ouvrieres, 101 (1971); see also Anton Pannekoek, *Workers' Councils* (Cambridge, Mass.: Root and Branch, 1970). For a critical examination of this area of Marx's thought, see John Crump, *A Contribution to the Critique of Marx* (London: Social Revolution/Solidarity, 1975).

Bibliography

Bragard, Jean-Claude, *An Investigation of Marxs Concept of Communism* (unpublished D Phil thesis, Oxford, 1981).

Burnham, James, *The Managerial Revolution* (London: Penguin, 1945).

Group of International Communists (GIC/GIKH), *Grundprinzipien Kommunistiche Verteilung und Produktion* (Berlin: AAUD, 1930).

Hayek, F. A. von et al., *Collectivist Economic Planning: Critical Studies on the Possibilities of Socialism* (London: Routledge, 1935).

Kautsky, K., *The Social Revolution* (Chicago: Kerr, 1902).

Mandel, Ernest, *Marxist Economic Theory* (London: Merlin, 1968).

Mans Dreams, *Mans Dreams Are Coming True* (Moscow: Progress Publishers, 1966).

Marx, Karl, *Capital*, 3 vols (Chicago: Kerr, 1919).

_____, *'Results of the Immediate Process of Production'* – Appendix to Marx, Karl, Capital, vol. I (Harmondsworth: Penguin, 1979)

Mises, Ludwig von, *Economic Calculation in the Socialist Commonwealth* in Hayek, F. A. et al (1935).

Neurath, Otto, *Wirtschaftsplan und Naturalrechnung* (Berlin: E. Laub, 1925).

Nove, Alec, *The Economics of Feasible Socialism* (London: George Allen & Unwin, 1983).

Pannekoek, Anton, *Workers Councils* (Detroit: Root and Branch, 1970).

Philoren, *Money Must Go* (London: J. Phillips, 1943).

Pierson, N. G., *The Problem of Value in the Socialist Society* in Hayek, F. A et al. (1935).

Samuelson, Paul, *Economics, an Introductory Analysis*, 11th ed (New York: McGraw-Hill, 1980).

Sherman, Howard J., *The Economics of Pure Communism in Soviet Studies*, XXII,1(1970).

Stonier, A. W; and Hague, DC, *A Textbook of Economic Theory*, 5th ed (London: Longmans, 1980).

Wallerstein, Immanuel, *The Capitalist World-Economy* (Cambridge University Press,1979)

Wiles, Peter, *The Political Economy of Communism* (Oxford: Blackwell, 1962).

www.ingramcontent.com/pod-product-compliance
Lightning Source LLC
Chambersburg PA
CBHW051031030426
42336CB00015B/2818